Tattered Cover
Book Store

The
Tattered
Cover
2823 East Second Avenue
Denver, Colorado 80206
(303) 322-7861
Stephen Cogil

books are the best friends you can have; they inform you and entertain you and don't talk back. John Steinbeck

TATTERED COVER

BOOKS

THE TATTERED COVER
2823 EAST SECOND AVE.
DENVER, COLORADO 80206
303-322-7727

Tattered Cover Book Store

A Storied History

Mark A. Barnhouse

THE
History
PRESS

Published by The History Press
Charleston, SC
www.historypress.com

Front cover: Joyce Meskis (*seated on chair, center*) with staff members in front of the original location, 1979. *Tattered Cover Archive.*
Back cover: The McGregor Square store, 2021. *Photograph by author; inset*: former first lady Michelle Obama with Tattered Cover staff members, Colfax store, 2018. *Tattered Cover Archive.*

Frontispiece: Throughout this book, Tattered Cover's free bookmarks tell the store's history. *Left*: Stephen Cogil's bookmarks, circa 1971–74, featured a geometric *T*. *Right*: After Joyce Meskis bought the store, she adopted a more homemade look with a drawing of the front window and Dutch door, circa 1975–79.

First published 2021

ISBN 9781540250599

Library of Congress Control Number: 2021945868

Notice: The information in this book is true and complete to the best of our knowledge. It is offered without guarantee on the part of the author or The History Press. The author and The History Press disclaim all liability in connection with the use of this book.

To Joyce Meskis,
who has given us a gift

Contents

Preface

A DIALOGUE

(telephone rings)

Tattered Cover Employee: Hello, this is _____, how may I help you?

Caller: Good morning. I'm calling from *Vanity Fair*, fact-checking a Dominick Dunne piece on the O.J. Simpson case.

Employee: Really?

Caller: Yes. Mr. Dunne spoke at your store several months ago, and in the article he claims that someone gave him a lead while he was signing books there.

Employee: Stranger things have happened!

Caller: I'm sure. He refers to it as "the legendary Tattered Cover Book Store."

Employee: My goodness!

Caller: The reason I'm calling is to find out if the store is really "legendary."

Employee: Well…

The dialogue is a reconstruction, but the fact is true: *Vanity Fair* really asked this question. Anyone who has ever shopped at Tattered Cover knows the answer: yes, indeed, it deserves its "legendary" reputation.

Since 1971, Tattered Cover Book Store has brought people and books together. Whether you grew up in Denver or just arrived, chances are that you have a Tattered Cover story to tell. Maybe you attended a midnight Harry Potter party, dressed in your PJs, sleepy but excited, planning to read until the sun came up to find out what happened to Harry, Hermione and Ron. Maybe you stood in line for hours to shake First Lady Hillary Clinton's hand or to ask Michael Hague to draw something. Maybe you stood in line in LoDo for hours to cast your 2004 vote, when that store served as polling place—or maybe you wrote a mystery novel whose opening scene takes place there. Maybe you came to meet David Foster Wallace, or Kurt Vonnegut, or Allen Ginsberg or Julia Child. Maybe Gloria Steinem inspired you when she ended her book signings with the command to "go out and raise trouble!" or Charlayne Hunter-Gault did when she spoke about desegregating the University of Georgia. Maybe you came to see your idols: Jimmy Carter, R. Buckminster Fuller, Jimmy Stewart, Kareem Abdul-Jabbar, Linda Ellerbee, Buzz Aldrin, John Glenn, Michelle Obama or Alice Walker. Maybe you came to see your favorite Colorado author: Clive Cussler, Sandra Dallas, Tom Noel, Helen Thorpe, John Fielder, Pam Houston, Opalonga Pugh, Ted Conover, Peter Heller, Manuel Ramos, Stephen White or Phil Goodstein. Maybe you laughed at Dave Barry, who may hold the record for the most Tattered Cover appearances, or at Rita Rudner or David Sedaris.

Or maybe you discovered your son was gay and needed a book or three to help you understand. Maybe you were a lesbian daughter and needed to figure out how to come out. Maybe your spouse died and you came seeking books on grieving. Maybe you were diagnosed with cancer and needed to know more than what your doctor told you. Maybe you were expecting your first child and needed to know what to expect when you were expecting. Maybe you were starting a business, or a new career, or were confused by Microsoft's Windows 95. Maybe you wanted to know how to bake bread, mix a drink, plant a xeriscape garden, plan a wedding, plan a trip to Japan, trace ancestors, remodel your kitchen, speak Portuguese or file taxes. Maybe you wanted to know more about the Civil War, existentialism, Sondheim, Gurdjieff or jazz. Maybe you needed a topographical map to plan a hike. Maybe you were seeking a magazine article, like Jon Krakauer's viral (before viral was a thing) *Outside* piece recounting deaths on Everest or *Spy*'s regular mockery of a certain small-handed New York developer. Maybe you were craving the Fourth Story's ravioli. Maybe you were just meeting friends for coffee. Tattered Cover has been there for you.

Children's author/illustrator Aliki Brandenberg drew this whimsical salute to Tattered Cover in the store's autograph book on a 1997 visit.

I have long thought of Tattered Cover as a holy place, a church of ideas. My own TC story began in 1980, when I read about it in *Westword* and decided I had to see why its editor considered it Denver's best bookstore. As years went by, I became, like so many Coloradans, a Tattered Cover habitué. As I was never one to borrow a book when I could buy one, the store garnered much of my income, sometimes too much. In my thirties, I began my own Tattered Cover career, the most interesting period of my life. I learned that the staff, not the inventory, was the store's greatest resource. Here were people with advanced degrees with encyclopedic knowledge and deep memories, people courted by publishers major and minor, people on a first-name basis with major authors, people who had devoted their lives to spreading ideas, engaged in creative activities of all kinds. Here were people who became important friends.

For help with this book I am indebted to many Tattered Cover people, past and present, including Christine Ashe, Bret Bertholf, Allie Bravo, Joanne Bruining, Sarah Clark, Heather Duncan, Alan Frosh, Ellen Hesdorfer, Derek Holland, Margie Keenan, Roy Laird, Kalen Landow, Cathy Langer, Jeff Lee, Ann Marie Martin, Jennifer Martin, Margaret Maupin, Linda Millemann, Matt Miller, Patty Miller, Molly Moyer, Jeremy Patlen, Andrea Phillips, Ron Plageman, Steve Radow, Donald Rae, Katherine Rose Rainbolt, Stacey Riegelhaupt, Tom Rowan, Laura Snapp, Kwame Spearman, Annita Spiker, Charles Stillwagon, Neil Strandberg, Matt Sullivan, Adam Vitcavage, Len Vlahos, Beth Wood and, of course, *and most of all*, Joyce Meskis. Without her thoughtfulness in 2009, when she received a phone call from an Arcadia Publishing editor looking for potential authors, I would never have had a career in writing and publishing books on Denver history. Thanks too to Artie Crisp at The History Press for thinking of me for this project, and to Reggie Ruth Barrett, Sandra Dallas, Abigail Fleming, Howie Movshovitz, Thomas J. Noel and Reed Weimer for their help. Finally, thanks as always to Matt Wallington, without whose influence on my life I may never have worked at Tattered Cover at all.

Note to readers: "1st Avenue Store" and "Cherry Creek Store" are synonymous. Unless otherwise indicated, all images are from the Tattered Cover Archive.

Part One

Fifty Years

I got into this business because I love books. I mean I really love books. *That, to me, is what running a bookstore is about. Publishing and books are incredibly important to humanity. I really believe that. I think if we don't fill our role of putting books in the hands of people who want to read them, it's almost sinful.*
—*Joyce Meskis, 1984*

A STORE IS BORN

Denver has always been a book town. It might seem curious to say that about a city far from Ivy League universities, but books began trading here as early as 1860, when David Moffat and Clarence Clarke opened the city's first book, stationery and cigar shop on 11th Street in Auraria. Over the decades, numerous bookstores satisfied Denver's literary needs, often lasting for years before fading away. In 1971, at 2823 East 2nd Avenue in Cherry Creek North, Denver native Stephen Cogil leased 950 square feet of retail space, the equivalent of a two-bedroom apartment, and opened a bookshop on the ground floor of a two-story building between Fillmore and Detroit Streets. A large multipaned window faced 2nd Avenue, and customers entered through a Dutch door, its top half often kept open on hot summer afternoons. Cogil hardly suspected that he was founding the most important bookselling institution in Denver's history—he just loved books and wanted to share his passion.

Cogil's dreams were not especially big. He stocked books that interested him, personally reading much of the inventory so he could recommend books he knew were good, and he wanted to offer unmatched personal service. In the early 1970s, his tiny shop was not unusual—Denver was dotted with small bookstores, including Pooh Corner at Cherry Creek Shopping Center, Bloomsbury Books near the University of Denver, Footnote in Larimer Square, Trilogy Books at 6th Avenue and Washington Street, Tumbleweed Books at 3rd Avenue and Holly Street and ABC Books & Posters at University Hills Plaza, to name a few. Technically, they competed with one another, but they also used one another as resources—if a customer sought a title a store did not stock, a clerk or owner would call another nearby store for them, a tradition the Tattered Cover followed even as the internet made finding hard-to-find books easy. In those days, too, the city's two major department stores, The Denver Dry Goods Company and May-D&F, still maintained robust book departments, and every supermarket and drugstore sold the latest mass-market paperbacks from wire spinner racks. Unlike those outlets, the original Tattered Cover offered a (necessarily) highly curated selection based on the interests of its owner. The shop struggled, and after three years Cogil decided to sell. Fortunately, he found a buyer.

THE OLD STORE

Joyce Meskis was not new to books or bookstores when she paid Cogil something under $30,000 for Tattered Cover. Born in Lansing, Illinois, in 1942, she grew up in Calumet City and Chicago's South Side, the daughter of a driver-salesman for Dolly Madison Bakery and granddaughter of a Lithuanian immigrant dairyman. Growing up in an ethnic neighborhood, she knew mostly local businesses: corner groceries, dress shops, bookshops, restaurants and taverns. Early on, she learned from relatives to "Sell More What Sells," known by generations of Tattered Cover employees as "SMoWS." In other words, know what your customers want and don't run out. She also learned the value of local businesses, because money spent there stayed in the community, rather than being siphoned off to distant corporate stockholders—when money circulates locally it benefits everyone. Upon entering Purdue University, Meskis set her sights on teaching mathematics as a career, but after switching her major to English and working in the library and college bookstore, she realized her true passion was books.

After closing Parker Book Shop, Meskis kept its wooden sign, hanging it above the original 2nd Avenue store's front door. It now resides in Tattered Cover's offices. *Photograph by author.*

In 1962, her first husband accepted a job in Colorado, and Meskis found work at Littleton Public Library and Englewood's The Book House. Her marriage ended, leaving her with about $7,000, and she decided to pursue her dream of opening her own bookstore. Parker, Colorado, settled in 1864 and twenty miles southeast of downtown, was poised by the late 1960s to become Denver's next bedroom suburb. The Parker City Land Company created a master plan for a community of over five thousand. To potential retailers, the developer promised that houses would soon fill the empty prairie, and Meskis thought the location, soon to be surrounded by families, was ideal, establishing the Parker Book Shop. Unfortunately, the land company soon went belly-up, but not before she had invested everything she had in inventory and fixtures. Faced with financial doom, she read that Cogil was selling Tattered Cover. Pulling together funds from every possible source, she scraped up enough to buy it. Cogil accepted another, higher offer, but Meskis's new interest Rudy Knauer (whom she later married) encouraged her to stay in contact with Cogil. When that higher bid evaporated, her persistence paid off. On Labor Day weekend in 1974, she and Knauer packed up the Parker stock and hauled it down to 2nd Avenue, combining it with Cogil's inventory. She hired her first employee, Joan Walther, a former library colleague who had contributed financially to Meskis's bid.

She soon ran out of room; this would not be the last time Tattered Cover required more space, and to create it she took out the store's restroom, relying on the kindness of nearby shops when nature called. Over several years, Meskis snapped up additional spots in the building as they became available, ultimately expanding six times to six thousand square feet. When the entire second floor opened up in 1978, she built a stairway, even though skeptical publishers' sales reps told her no one would climb it. She hired more booksellers. The store began to acquire a reputation for its breadth and depth

Opposite: The original store's south-facing front window.

This page, top: The earliest staff photograph, in front of the original store, 1979.

This page, bottom: Skepticism abounded when Meskis had stairs built in 1978, but thousands had climbed them by the time of this December 1982 photograph.

Opposite, top: The staff posed on the stairs, 1979.

Opposite, bottom: The original store was especially busy during the holidays, 1982.

Above: Lavish art calendars hung from the stairway railing, because every square foot counted, 1984.

of inventory: not only did this "general interest" bookstore carry something for everyone, but it also stocked a great many titles in every category. Books were everywhere, stacked under tables and filling spaces between the tops of bookcases and the ceiling. But the store was not arranged in parallel aisles, as in a library: instead, it comprised, as Tattered Cover still does today, a series of rooms or nooks. Someone on staff—Meskis never took credit herself—realized that customers bought more books the longer they stayed, and standing was not conducive to lingering. Rather than have shoppers sit on the shag-carpeted floor, comfortable chairs, with adjacent reading lamps, were necessary, and Meskis combed through antique shops, searching for pieces that resembled furniture in her parents' house. A tradition was born: when chain book "superstores" arose in the 1980s and 1990s, they copied this idea of comfortable seating from Tattered Cover, but never as authentically.

THE MIDDLE STORE

Nine years after she bought Tattered Cover, it needed yet more room, and Meskis took another large risk, leasing a nearly eleven-thousand-square-foot space one block east on the opposite (southern) side of 2nd Avenue. This was in a newly constructed addition to the Neusteters parking garage with two levels of storefronts, one at sidewalk level and one below grade, stretching from Fillmore to Milwaukee Streets. Tattered Cover occupied a small ground-level space at 2930 East 2nd Avenue, midway between the two streets, and a much larger space below, connected with a bookshelf-lined staircase. Meskis kept the original location too, now designated the "Old Store," giving the operation a combined seventeen thousand square feet. With the new store housing more than forty departments, at the old one, customers shopped for "bargain books," often the prior year's hardcovers steeply marked down by publishers once paperback versions arrived. This was new for Tattered Cover, which previously lacked space for anything but regular-price books. The new store was to have opened in the fall of 1982, but construction delays forestalled the move until after the holiday shopping season. However, bargain books, ordered in anticipation of creating the Bargain Store prior to the holidays, began arriving, boxes piled high. The only solution was to increase the size of the Old Store one last time: Meskis removed an office door and put up shelves. Immediately, she and store manager Matt Miller, who had created the bargain operation,

Left: Hundreds of customers helped Tattered Cover move into the Middle Store in January 1983.

Below: The Middle Store's open doors dressed for the holidays, 1984. These doors were the basis for the logo Tattered Cover still uses today. In 1986, they were reinstalled on the Milwaukee side of the 1st Avenue store.

Over the decades, *Garfield* books have been perennial favorites for readers of a certain age, circa 1983.

Browsers on the Middle Store's lower level, circa 1983.

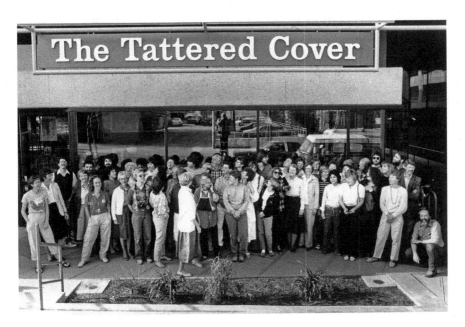

The staff posed in front of the Middle Store, circa 1986.

knew they had a winner, when eager buyers, some not able to afford full-price hardcovers, snapped up the new offerings. The Old Store, once the Middle Store opened, also carried an expanded selection of greeting cards, journals and other nonbook items along with an ever-growing newsstand of magazines and newspapers, many from other states and countries. When the new space was ready, on January 24, 1983, volunteers moved the books one block east—about three hundred customers, already intensely loyal to what they perceived as a bookstore above all others, were only too happy to help. This became a longstanding tradition.

THE CHERRY CREEK STORE:
A DEPARTMENT STORE FOR BOOKS

Yet even as Denver's economy cratered following the crash of the late 1970s–early 1980s oil boom, Tattered Cover continued growing, and Meskis sought even more space. In 1986, the opportunity presented itself. Longstanding fashion specialty store Neusteters, having undergone bankruptcy, was down to one location, at the opposite end of the block from Tattered Cover, and in March of that year it shuttered (see sidebar).

SUDDENLY A LARGE BUILDING with four levels, fronting busy 1st Avenue, became available, and Meskis took another huge gamble, leasing the entire building at 2955 East 1st Avenue save for its top floor, then occupied by a restaurant, The Chrysler. Keep in mind: Denver was shrinking, with more people moving out than moving in. New downtown skyscrapers sat mostly empty; Denver's office vacancy rate was the nation's highest and its lease rates the lowest. Unemployment was high and growing. Was Meskis crazy? Hardly. After about six hundred customers again volunteered to help the store move from the Old and Middle Stores, Tattered Cover became a "thing to see," immediately successful from the time it opened just before the 1986 holiday season. To paraphrase a line from one of that era's popular movies, she built it, and people came. Although it had been growing quietly and continuously since 1974, Denver suddenly boasted a landmark bookstore, noticed nationally. In 1987, *The New York Times* profiled Tattered Cover, describing it as "a 41,700-square-foot cornucopia of more than 400,000 books ranging from the Loeb Classical Library of Latin and Greek to books on channeling and spiritual healing," praising its

NEUSTETERS

The Cherry Creek Tattered Cover occupied what had been The Neusteter Company's most profitable branch. Founded in 1911 by three brothers from St. Louis, Max, Edward and Meyer Neusteter, the specialty store (the family's preferred term—they would not call their high-end operation a "department store") for decades served customers from 16th and Stout Streets. In 1958, recognizing the concentration of affluent customers living near Cherry Creek Shopping Center, it announced it would build across 1st Avenue from it. The branch, designed by Denver architect Paul Reddy, opened in 1960; the adjacent garage held five hundred cars. A fourth-floor restaurant and bar ("The Penthouse") operated by restaurateur Joe Shaner, served lunch and dinner, frequently hosting fashion shows. The opulent store included a Mr. Mack beauty salon and a Van Cleef & Arpels jewelry boutique. In the early 1980s, Meyer's grandson William helmed the company, and to revive its reputation he launched major renovations downtown and at Cherry Creek, where Reddy's crushed white marble façade gave way to a new earth-toned aggregate; Neusteter Realty also extended the garage to 2nd Avenue, its retail space housing the Middle Store. A family feud and Denver's post—oil boom recession spelled the end, with Neusteters closing stores until only Cherry Creek remained. In May 1986, it shuttered, and six months later Tattered Cover opened. After Tattered Cover moved to East Colfax Avenue in 2006, the landlord renovated, replacing aggregate with glass.

On August 29, 1960, well-dressed guests enjoyed the Cherry Creek Neusteters grand opening party, here in the second-floor fur department. *Photograph by Sandra Dallas; Tattered Cover Archive.*

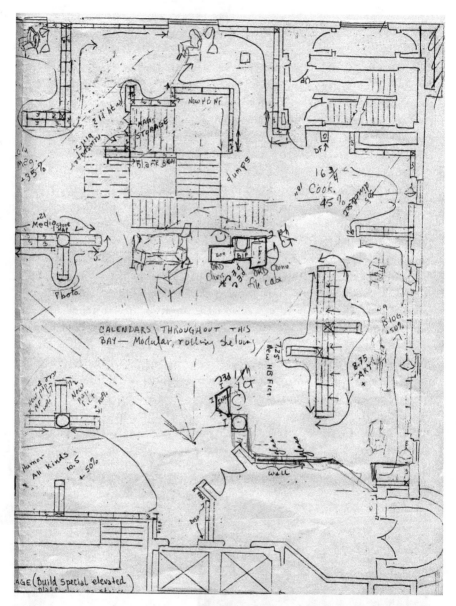

Joyce Meskis spent hours laying out each store she opened, usually with hand-drawn floor plans complete with chairs, tables and lamps. She made this early drawing of Cherry Creek's first floor in 1986, changing some aspects prior to opening. She also sometimes used LEGO blocks to design bookshelf arrangements. *Courtesy of Linda Millemann.*

When Cherry Creek opened in 1986, it required six miles of pine shelving. Ron Dirlam (not pictured) supervised installation and continued to do the same for every new Tattered Cover through Westminster.

Cherry Creek Tattered Cover, with attached parking garage, circa 1995.

"labyrinth of accessible nooks and crannies, where browsers can settle into overstuffed armchairs and couches." The furniture, along with wall-to-wall forest green carpeting, lent the store a homelike appeal. Less noticeable, perhaps, were the shelves and other display fixtures, constructed from inexpensive pine, stained dark brown to allow the books to visually "pop." Meskis wanted books to shine, not the décor, and when computerization became inevitable, after originally relying on thousands of index cards to track inventory, she had CRT monitors and keyboards painted dark brown. This might have invalidated their warranty, but it made them less visually prominent, which was paramount.

Customers entered through three street-level entrances, on Milwaukee Street, on 1st Avenue and from a pedestrian passageway. Those coming by car entered the second or third floors directly from the parking garage; Tattered Cover gave two hours' validation, regardless of whether someone bought something, a costly policy but absolutely necessary to Meskis. A cash counter occupied the center of the first floor, with four registers open daily, six on weekends and more during the holidays, when lines ran five and six people deep. Another cash counter on the second floor served customers picking up books at the Reserve Desk, which typically saw several hundred customers daily, picking up special orders or books reserved by staffers when customers called seeking in-stock titles. Also on two were the store's giftwrap desk—no purchase was too small for free giftwrapping—and the "School and Corporate" department, which sold books in bulk. During the holidays, a third cash counter was rolled onto the third floor, allowing shoppers to exit to the garage without having to brave the crowds below. At the south end, a grand stairway, broken by bookshelf-lined landings, connected the three open-to-the-public floors; patrons could also ride two elevators.

As originally configured, the first floor housed new hardcover and paperback fiction and nonfiction; art and photography; biography; Colorado history; crafts, cookbooks, humor and games; business and computers; reference; music; and an extensive newsstand that wrapped around the staircase's rear side. With over 1,200 titles, the newsstand was one of Denver's most extensive, and its selection of over 30 out-of-state Sunday newspapers became an important destination for people seeking jobs in other cities. Foreign papers attracted expatriates wanting news from home. On two were religion, philosophy, psychology, gender studies, nature, science, animals, sports, health, architecture and interior design, and bargain books, a vast selection categorized into the same departments

At right, longtime employees Matt and Patty Miller pose inside Cherry Creek's 1st Avenue entry, which featured her trompe l'oeil mural on its curved walls. Below, the 1st Avenue entrance on a snowy day, date unknown.

This page: Cherry Creek's first floor. Above, view from the stair landing toward the cash counter. Below, looking from the same landing toward the cookbook, biography and art sections; both, circa 1992.

This page: Cherry Creek's second-floor philosophy (*above*) and psychology (*below*) sections. Note the psychiatrist couch on the left in the lower photograph; both, circa 1992.

This page: Cherry Creek's third floor. Above, the view from the author signing area. Below, the top of the staircase, with a narrow walkway behind lined with history books; both, circa 1992.

as the non-bargain sections. On three, a large open space hosted book signings, soon a near-daily occurrence. Also on three were fiction sections (literary, science fiction and fantasy, horror and romance), poetry, literary criticism, reference, performing arts (theater, film, television), history, sociology, politics, globes and maps, travel, foreign language, parenting and children's. Here too were a small number of Braille titles and books on tape, along with the Loeb Library that had so impressed *The New York Times*.

Later, after Meskis moved back-of-house operations off site, contractors removed a wall that obscured a stairway at the north end of the first floor. It had led Neusteters shoppers to the "Garden Level," and it now connected Tattered Cover customers to the "Lower Level" (Meskis's preferred term—staffers were discouraged from saying "basement"). This necessitated significant reconfiguration. To the Lower Level went bargain books, business, computers and children's, where high, excited voices would no longer disturb people assembled on three to hear authors read. History came down to the first floor. Other departments remained on their original

Cherry Creek's new paperback fiction and nonfiction sections occupied prime space near the stairs, circa 1992. These four bookcases probably sold more books than any other four in the store and required replenishment several times daily.

Above and opposite top: Views of Cherry Creek's famous stairway. Above, midway between the second and third floors. Opposite, top, midway between the first and second floors; both, circa 1992.

Stairs to the Lower Level, circa 2006.

Cherry Creek's stairway landings were lined with books, including theme displays such as this one for Black History Month, 1998. Staff artist Sarah Clark was responsible for most of these, producing great effects with a limited budget.

Cherry Creek's popular lower-level bargain department, circa 1992.

floors, expanded to fill newly available space. Another reconfiguration occurred in 1994, when the store added its first foodservice operation, a coffee bar that proved far more popular than Cherry Creek North's chain coffee shops. In 1995, Meskis hired professional restaurateur Chris Golub to open Fourth Story Restaurant & Bar, an upscale eatery on the fourth floor, occupying what had been restaurant space for most of the building's history, except for a few years when it housed offices and book storage. Fourth Story's large windows looked south, with Pikes Peak visible sixty miles away; bookshelves offered popular titles that diners could add to their tab.

It Takes a Village to Run a Bookstore

There was more to Tattered Cover than met the eye. Behind the scenes staffers performed myriad functions beyond simply receiving books. A buying staff chose titles in the frontlist (newly published books), midlist (solid sellers from lesser-known authors) and backlist (older books, still in print) categories. For

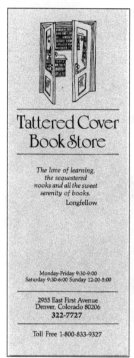

Tattered Cover Book Store

*The love of learning,
the sequestered
nooks and all the sweet
serenity of books.*
Longfellow

Monday-Friday 9:30-9:00
Saturday 9:30-6:00 Sunday 12:00-5:00

2955 East First Avenue
Denver, Colorado 80206
322-7727

Toll Free 1-800-833-9327

**Tattered Cover
Book Store**

*"The love of learning,
the sequestered nook
and all the sweet
serenity of books."*
Longfellow

Monday thru Saturday 9:30 to 9:00
Sunday 10:00 to 6:00

♦ ♦ ♦

2955 East First Avenue
Denver, Colorado 80206
(303) 322-7727 (800) 833-9327
FAX (303) 399-2279

a small fee, specialists in rare and out-of-print books searched for titles requested by customers. Other specialists ordered from foreign publishers, for the store's foreign language section and for customers seeking particular titles. The store's "Mail and Bill" (later renamed "Customer Shipping") department located books on store shelves, packed them and shipped them to anyone who phoned or faxed in an order. In-store customers could also have books shipped this way, handy for tourists buying more than would fit into their luggage and for people buying for out-of-state gift-giving. Books are typically returnable to publishers for credit; the returns department shipped titles that had been on the shelves too long. A physical operations team moved books from place to place—on carts to store departments and in the store's box truck, picking up daily orders from a local wholesaler.

When a customer dialed either the store's local or toll-free number, an operator answered. During the day, two or three people sat in a small room answering calls from twenty-six lines and routing them to the appropriate section; if no bookseller answered, the operator would keep trying until someone could help the customer. During the holidays, with gift certificates sold over the phone, people worked phone shifts performing just that task. The store also owned a TTY device to communicate with non-hearing customers. Meskis believed most people were basically honest, so if someone paid by check the cashier would not ask for identification; rarely did any checks bounce. Meskis also believed most people would pay their bills, and established house accounts for anyone

These bookmarks show the evolution of Tattered Cover's graphics, both incorporating the "Open Door" logo. Top, circa 1987. Bottom, circa 1992.

"Charlie" (*left, wearing party hat*) has been a beloved Tattered Cover presence since Joyce Meskis purchased the fiberglass sculpture by Denver artist Quang Ho in 1990. Modeled after real-life Charlie Shugarts (*right*, seen here at an eighty-fourth birthday celebration in 2002), "Charlie" typically was found reading a newspaper held in outstretched hands. Shugarts, who died in 2007, loved surprising people by posing next to himself.

who asked, without credit checks. Accounts payable and receivable staffs processed invoices and billed customers. There were also an art department, an IT team, a coordinator and team running events, a scheduler and a marketing team to create newsletters and publicize the store's author visits and other events.

To land a Tattered Cover job you had to demonstrate you could listen. During the interview, a member of the personnel team would talk and talk and talk. If you listened, you were hired. If you interrupted frequently, you were not a good candidate. When someone was hired, they went through extensive training before encountering customers. Trainees learned to perform any transaction that might come up and were shown how to act. Meskis spent a day with each new training group, recounting the store's history and imparting her philosophies of bookselling and freedom of ideas. In an instructional video, employees portrayed various roles, demonstrating good, bad and "okay" customer interactions. Central to the training was discretion: no customer should ever feel self-conscious about a book they bought, and no customer should ever feel the bookseller

This page: Cherry Creek's coffee bar opened in the fall of 1994. Meskis specified it must brew coffee from Colorado roasters, and when the store's purveyor, Boulder-based Allegro, sold to a Texas-based natural grocery chain, the coffee bar switched to a Vail-based roaster.

considered them ignorant or unintelligent. Quiet voices were better than overenthusiastic responses to queries. The person in front of you required your full attention—if someone else needed help, tell that customer they would be helped soon and look for another staffer to step in. Do not say the book is "over there," pointing with your finger—take them to the shelf and put the book in their hand. Always offer to order the book if it was not in stock. Allow students to plop down and take notes from books without buying—they would become local customers later. New staffers worked cash registers exclusively for several months; only after they had "graduated" from this period could they work as booksellers on the floor. Boston-based publisher David R. Godine told the *Rocky Mountain News*, "Harvard Business School should have the Joyce Meskis endowed chair of customer service and common sense."

Harvard Business School might have taken issue with Meskis's management style, however, as it did not resemble any traditional model. In early years, with about 25 employees it was "all hands on deck" per longtime employee Roy Laird—everyone did everything in an unstructured way. As the store grew to about 130 employees by the mid-1980s and ultimately to more than 400 by the mid-1990s, Meskis faced pressure to create structure. She resisted but ultimately adopted a system where general managers oversaw particular operational areas. Additionally, she created store manager and floor manager positions. Even with this arrangement, she endeavored to retain a sense of community among the staff. Public-facing employees understood it was best to err on the side of generosity and service, per former general manager Linda Millemann. Neil Strandberg, Cherry Creek store manager in the 1990s and 2000s, saw Meskis's style as a kind of critique of capitalism as it had been practiced by the business mainstream: employees were not disposable, and each person added value.

Meskis created a safe haven for her employees, which attracted many creative types who did not always fit into traditional offices or rigid workplaces. This included many LGBTQ+ staffers, hired when it was still legal in Colorado to fire members of these communities for their sexual orientations or gender identities. The store lost a number of gay men to the AIDS pandemic prior to the discovery of treatment regimens and gained a reputation for its gay-friendliness and support. In 1992, shortly after Colorado voters passed Amendment 2, an anti-LGBTQ initiative that banned local governments from enacting job protection ordinances, a store switchboard operator received a threatening phone call. "You have too

This page: Fourth Story Restaurant & Bar, circa 1995.

Tattered Cover employees used to wear pins; more recently staffers have worn custom lanyards. *Photograph by author.*

Opposite, top: Volunteers helping Tattered Cover move always got free commemorative T-shirts. Here are two, from 1986 (*left*) and 2006, a contest winner (*right*). *Photograph by author.*

Opposite, bottom: Tattered Cover employees are avid readers, composing handwritten shelf tags to express admiration for their favorite books.

Above: In the 1990s, Rocky Mountain Book Festival took place in (now demolished) Currigan Hall downtown, and Tattered Cover participated with pop-up stores. Note "Charlie" perched on a bookcase, circa 1995.

many f—s [expletive deleted] working there," the caller said. "You're going to pay with a bomb." There was no explosive device—it was a cowardly, empty threat. The store called 911, evacuated customers and employees and, the next day, carried on as usual, unbowed and unintimidated by intolerance.

THE HISTORIC LODO STORE: BRIGHT IDEAS

In 1990, Joyce Meskis needed more space for back-of-house operations and offices. Cherry Creek was overcrowded, and nearby leased spaces at Cherry Creek Shopping Center and in the empty Joseph Magnin store on Fillmore Street were only temporary solutions. LoDo (lower downtown), a district of muscular, old, brick, multistory warehouses built in the late nineteenth and early twentieth centuries, intrigued her. She knew one person who had already pioneered the area, a tall, thin, gawky-looking man named John Hickenlooper. Three years earlier, this unemployed oil geologist bought an old warehouse at 18th and Wynkoop Streets, spent thousands on renovation and opened a brewpub in it, with beer made on site. The Wynkoop Brewing Company was as talked about as Tattered Cover, a place people took out-of-town relatives to demonstrate Denver's innovative spirit. She told him what she needed, and late on Valentine's Day, he knocked on her door with a short list of available properties, which he had assembled with commercial broker Charles Woolley. Hickenlooper described his idea to bring in retail activity and affordable housing and proposed partnering with Meskis on a project that would incorporate her needs for a back-of-house facility, a possible second Tattered Cover and housing for underpaid downtown workers.

Hickenlooper's first choice, a property originally built for Denver Tramway Company at 17th and Wynkoop on the same block as his brewpub, was shortly snapped up by developers for luxury lofts—the LoDo property market was heating up as people began recognizing its potential. One block southwest at 1628 16th Street was the former C.S. Morey Mercantile Company, a blond-brick six-story warehouse built in 1896 for Chester Morey, a grocery wholesaler (see sidebar).

Nearby at 1536 Wynkoop Street was another six-story structure, its early 1980s renovation financed by Pueblo's Otero Savings and Loan. It was now owned by Resolution Trust Corporation, the entity created by

C.S. MOREY MERCANTILE COMPANY

Chester Stephen Morey, born in Wisconsin in 1847, fought for the Union in the Civil War, seeing action at Petersburg and present for Lee's surrender at Appomattox Court House. Afterward, he engaged in retail groceries in Chicago, where Meskis's relations would later ply the same trade. Coming to Colorado in 1872 for his health, in 1884 he founded his namesake firm. When he built his six-story warehouse at 1628 16th Street in 1896, he demonstrated his faith in Denver, confident it would bounce back from the Panic of 1893. Its ground floor was elevated, the height matching railroad boxcar floors. Rail spurs on Wynkoop and on the double-width alley allowed cars to load and unload directly. The 16th Street viaduct blocked the first floor from sunlight, so architects Aaron Gove and Thomas Walsh put the main entrance on the second floor, where offices were located; when the viaduct came down in 1993, the second-floor entry was marooned in midair. In 1907, Morey bought the Henry Lee building, spanning the alley with bridges. Morey also produced a line of packaged goods under the Solitaire label, familiar to all Colorado cooks of that era. Neighborhood and small-town grocers who bought from Morey sported metal storefront signage reading "Home-Owned Stores" with a Solitaire logo; one of these decorated Tattered Cover's second-floor bridge. Morey was even-tempered, but when he saw a body drop down the open elevator shaft he nearly had a heart attack. When he discovered it was a young employee showing off his derring-do, sliding down the cable instead of walking downstairs, he fired him. The youth, a Denver native named Douglas Fairbanks, later became Hollywood's most bankable male movie star. Morey Mercantile lasted until 1956; in later years the building was a warehouse.

Aerial view of future Mercantile Square, circa 1990. Note the 16th Street viaduct, lower left, with its connection to the future Tattered Cover's second floor.

the George H.W. Bush administration to manage properties financed by America's many defunct savings and loan companies. Between these was another old red brick building that Morey had owned, and across the alley, connected by bridges, was a fourth building that was once part of Morey's operation and had originally been built by farm implement dealer Henry Lee. Two parking lots, one adjacent to what soon came to be called the "Otero Building," and another on Wazee across 16th from the "Henry Lee Building," completed what Hickenlooper, Meskis and partners dubbed "Mercantile Square."

For this now much more complicated project Meskis left financial aspects to Hickenlooper, who with partners assembled a complex mix of funding sources. They won a grant from Denver Urban Renewal Authority for the housing component and state historic preservation tax credits for the renovation. As originally envisioned, Mercantile Square would combine Tattered Cover's back-of-house with a second bookstore, other locally owned businesses, workforce housing, a daycare center and a charter school that would incorporate urban experiences into its curriculum. (The daycare and school were later dropped.) As pieces began coming together, Tattered Cover's receiving operations transitioned to the Lee Building and its offices moved into the Otero. The partners hired Denver architect David Owen

When LoDo opened, everything was compact, including its cash counter.

LoDo's coffee bar, circa 1997.

Tryba to design the renovation plan, and in 1993 the city demolished the aging 16th Street viaduct for a planned 16th Street Mall extension. A few blocks to the northeast, Coors Field began rising, bringing Major League Baseball to LoDo. Suddenly, this corner of downtown was taking off—the partners had bought at just the right time. Upper floors became a mix of market-rate and income-qualified apartments (some tenanted by store employees), and local businesses Dixon's restaurant and Wines Off Wynkoop in the Lee Building joined Tattered Cover.

The LoDo Tattered Cover opened its doors in October 1994, a single floor at first, while upper floors underwent renovation. Meskis opened it then also because she was negotiating new lease terms with her Cherry Creek landlord, and if she could not get a low-enough rate to remain

Opposite, top: Joyce Meskis stands, right, in LoDo's history room, a repurposed loading dock, circa 1999.

Opposite, bottom: LoDo's stairway, patterned after Cherry Creek's, with bookshelves on landings, 2011.

Above: LoDo's second floor, circa 2008.

viable there she told that landlord she would move the entire operation to LoDo. (Her strategy worked). Two years later, a large staircase modeled after Cherry Creek's connected the ground floor with the second and third, and an elevator rose nearby. This thirty-five-thousand-square foot store was clearly Tattered Cover, but it was not like Cherry Creek. While interior walls were painted dark brown like the older store, exterior walls were exposed red brick. The first floor was not carpeted; instead, the original wooden floor, its stripped and refinished planks laid diagonally, cast a warm glow. The second and third floors were green-carpeted, due to fire regulations (a thin layer of concrete had to cover the original wooden floors). Thick timber columns cut from old-growth forests in the 1890s, stripped of layers of pistachio green paint, rose to wooden ceilings. Many windows were original, noticeably wavy due to age. On the second and third floors, original fireplaces, newly outfitted with gas, occupied the 16th and Wynkoop corner. The second-floor alley bridge became the store's Event Hall, easily accommodating more than one hundred. The portion of this room closest to 16th Street had been Chester Morey's own office, boasting another fireplace; it became a "Morey Museum" with a portrait of him and collection of Morey Mercantile photographs and artifacts. On the main floor, Tryba created glass-enclosed spaces on former alley-facing loading docks.

Departments were arranged similarly to Cherry Creek, with some differences. Children's was on three, along with bargain books, fiction, performing arts, art and photography. The second floor housed psychology, religion, business, computers, nature, science and similar subject areas. The first floor included new hardcover and paperback fiction and nonfiction, cookbooks, humor and games and greeting cards. One of the enclosed docks was devoted to travel, maps and globes, while the other was filled with history books. A large newsstand boasting approximately two thousand magazines and newspapers occupied a large space adjacent to the coffee bar. As in Cherry Creek, the store was filled with interesting antique

LoDo's third-floor bargain section, circa 1997.

Staff artists Patty Miller and Ann Marie Martin hand-painted and stained this chess table to honor Lester Durrant, a homeless man known as "Sarge" who frequented LoDo, loved chess and got to know the staff. He passed away in the store in 2002, and then-manager Ernie Garrison conceived of this memorial to him; it now graces McGregor Square.

furniture, including a psychiatrist's couch in psychology and theater seating in performing arts.

Timing for a store this large was years early—Meskis had envisioned more business than was coming, and new competition was making bookselling more difficult. An aggressive new online retailer began eating away at every bookseller's sales, and the two large book superstore chains continued opening new branches across the Denver area (see sidebar). While LoDo came alive during baseball games and on weekend evenings, it was not yet the daytime destination it became after the 2014 reopening of Union Station as multimodal transit hub. This end of downtown felt like the edge, not the center; empty acres behind Union Station were a

COMPETITION AND LOCALISM

In 1984, in an all-store meeting Joyce Meskis voiced her worry that a national chain book superstore, Crown Books, would open several locations across Denver. Competition was not new: while the feared Crown invasion never came, national chains Waldenbooks and B. Dalton Bookseller were already in every mall. In 1990, Cherry Creek (mall) opened across 1st Avenue with three chain bookstores: Brentano's, Doubleday and Doubleday Travel, but they eventually closed because they could not compete with Tattered Cover. More significant competition arrived with multiple suburban Barnes & Noble stores. When in 1994 that chain opened on South Colorado Boulevard, just a mile or so from Cherry Creek, dips in traffic and sales were noticeable but not devastating. Later that decade, Borders Books & Music arrived. These brick-and-mortar stores did not hurt Tattered Cover as much as feared; Denver's metropolitan population was growing, enlarging the market. When Seattle-based Amazon began selling books online, however, the game changed. Although now it sells anything, in its early years it focused on books, something its founder viewed as a commodity anyone could hawk, replacing the hand-selling and personal recommendations stores like Tattered Cover specialized in with ever-more sophisticated algorithms. It now retails more than half of all books sold, an unprecedented share. In response, publishers have merged for bargaining clout and independent bookstores like Tattered Cover have banded together to promote buying locally.

When longtime Denverites mourn the relocation of the Cherry Creek Tattered Cover, their feelings are perfectly understandable—people also miss many other vanished landmarks. But it was the product of a particular time and set of circumstances that cannot be replicated. One: Denver's economy was so dire that the landlord was willing to risk leasing to a woman-owned bookstore at an affordable rate. Two: chain superstores did not greatly affect the store's business in its early years. Three: the Internet was in its infancy, not yet the retail marketplace it became. Four: Denver commercial real estate grew far more expensive thanks to the strong regional economy and related population boom. By 2010, three Tattered Cover stores (Colfax, LoDo, Highlands Ranch) saw combined annual sales of only about one-third of what Cherry Creek reached at its pre-Amazon peak. The best way to assuage nostalgic feelings for Cherry Creek (or LoDo) is to shop at today's several Tattered Cover locations or order from TatteredCover.com. Every purchase ensures the store will continue to serve Coloradans. More Americans are realizing they lose something important when they don't buy from local bookstores, hardware stores, clothing shops and other retailers. When money is spent locally it recirculates, benefiting the retailer, its employees and the community.

Customers relax on Cherry Creek's first floor, circa 1992.

no-man's land. After 2000, Meskis made the difficult decision to close the third floor, subleasing it as office space. In 2015, with Mercantile Square's ownership changed (Hickenlooper had divested when he first ran for political office), the store was given short notice to consolidate everything to the first floor; the landlord had found a tenant for the second. The stairway came out, and after a few chaotic months, a new, single-floor Tattered Cover emerged, only slightly larger than it had been in 1994. In April 2020, with one year left on its lease, the store announced it would move in spring 2021 to McGregor Square, the new development adjacent to Coors Field being built by Dick Monfort, owner of the Colorado Rockies baseball team, and on March 17, 2021, LoDo closed its doors. It

LoDo's third-floor fiction section, circa 1997.

lives on in fiction: in 2017, Matthew J. Sullivan , who worked in LoDo in the 1990s, published *Midnight at the Bright Ideas Bookstore*, a mystery whose opening scene, set in a fictionalized Tattered Cover, complete with wooden columns and views from third-floor windows of Union Station's "Travel by Train" sign, vividly recalls its atmosphere.

THE COLFAX STORE: THEATER OF IDEAS

By the early 2000s, the Cherry Creek North shopping district was changing. The 1990 opening of enclosed shopping mall "Cherry Creek" across 1st Avenue, anchored by new-to-Denver luxury stores Neiman Marcus, Saks Fifth Avenue and Lord & Taylor and Colorado stalwart May-D&F, radically increased property values and lease rates across the district. After the tumultuous 1980s, Denver saw the onset of a multidecade boom. Meskis was once again faced with negotiating with a money-minded landlord, but this time, the property owner wanted more than she could possibly afford and she had little leverage. Few realize how thin margins are for bookstores—books can be returned for credit,

This page: Two views of Colfax, 2021. *Photographs by author.*

A ramp lined with Bonfils/Lowenstein theatrical memorabilia leads to the "orchestra pit," 2021. *Photograph by author.*

but first they have to be paid for, labor is expensive and any change in lease rates can change black ink to red. Independent bookstores faced ever-increasing e-commerce and chain competition. Tattered Cover had to move from 1st and Milwaukee if it was to continue bringing people and books together.

Fortunately, after three decades as a leading Denver businesswoman, Meskis was well connected. Working again with developer Charles Woolley, whose St. Charles Town Company specialized in unusual renovation projects, she announced in January 2006 that the store would relocate approximately two miles north-northwest to the long-empty Bonfils-Lowenstein Theatre on East Colfax Avenue and Elizabeth Street (see sidebar).

Just as Tattered Cover had anchored the revitalizations of Cherry Creek and LoDo, it would catalyze East Colfax Avenue, the city's storied commercial strip now fallen on hard times. In the theater's former parking lot, Woolley built a three-hundred-car parking garage with retail spaces at street level. Unlike Cherry Creek, parking would be free, removing a huge financial burden from the store. Joining Tattered Cover would be independent music retailer Twist & Shout, its owner Paul Epstein similarly

BONFILS MEMORIAL THEATRE AND LOWENSTEIN THEATRE

Nobody loved theater as much as Helen Gilmer Bonfils, daughter of *Denver Post* co-publisher Frederick G. Bonfils. The wealthy heiress had produced plays and acted from her days at Miss Wolcott's School and as company member at Elitch Theatre. In 1929, Denver Civic Theatre, a nonprofessional community group, formed, performing at various venues. In the early 1950s, supporter Helen Bonfils bought land at East Colfax Avenue at Elizabeth Street and spent $1.25 million on Bonfils Memorial Theatre, honoring her father and mother, Belle. Designed by John K. Monroe in Art Moderne style, it was of blond brick, with pink marble at the entrance. The Colfax-fronting lobby featured pink-tinted windows with etched designs. The house sat 550; the basement accommodated an intimate cabaret and bar boasting the first liquor license granted to a Denver performing arts venue. The Bonfils opened on October 14, 1953, and operated into the 1980s. After Bonfils Foundation focused on the Denver Performing Arts Complex, it removed the Bonfils name from the Colfax theater to use for the downtown facility. In 1985, it renamed the Colfax venue for Henry Lowenstein, who had overseen more than four hundred productions. After one year as Lowenstein Theatre, it closed, and Lowenstein moved productions to a onetime cinema on Santa Fe Drive, reviving the name Denver Civic Theatre (now Su Teatro). The building sat empty from 1986 until its conversion into Tattered Cover.

Bonfils
Theatre,
circa 1953.

Above: Bonfils Theatre's lobby, transformed into Tattered Cover's newsstand, circa 2006.

Opposite: Stairs to Colfax's lower level retain original architectural features, 2021. *Photograph by author.*

committed, like Meskis, to deep selection, excellent service, local artists and in-store events. Joining them were an art cinema (now Sie Film Center), the Denver Folklore Center and restaurants. It is not a stretch to say that the presences of Tattered Cover and the others greatly helped transform the stretch of Colfax from Gaylord Street east to Colorado Boulevard, now lined with many more interesting shops and restaurants than were present in 2006.

Five months after the announcement, customers (including the author) again volunteered to help the store move on the last weekend of June, packing up books in Cherry Creek and unpacking and shelving them in their new home. The twenty-four-thousand-square foot store became another instant landmark. Because the building is historic, many of its original details remained, including dramatic etched-glass lobby windows facing the Sullivan Gateway across Colfax, seating boxes at the auditorium's rear wall, the orchestra pit, the stage and the proscenium, rehung with a red velvet valence. Architect Jeffrey Stine of Lawrence Group Architects, an adaptive reuse specialist firm, designed the renovation plan. Most book departments occupied the main floor, now flat instead of sloped, and the stage, where the reserve desk was also placed, easily accessed from the rear parking lot. A coffee bar adjoined the entry facing Twist & Shout. Down twin stairways that connected the original lobby with Bonfils Theatre's Bo-Ban's Cabaret and coat check were children's books, sports, foreign language, travel and maps, nature and science, surrounding the author event space. Underneath the auditorium, onetime scenery and costume fabrication shops and actors' dressing rooms now housed shipping, receiving and offices.

ADDING LEAVES TO THE BOOK

In addition to the two large Denver stores, Colfax and LoDo, the twenty-first century saw Tattered Cover respond to the city's evolution by opening additional locations, each evoking the feeling of the original stores. Each was also a gamble, but as longtime general manager Matt Miller told a *Denver Post* reporter, "Sometimes it's a greater risk not to grow." The first was at Highlands Ranch Town Center, at South Broadway, Highlands Ranch Parkway and Lucent Boulevard, where a twenty-two-thousand-square foot store opened in November 2004. The mix was slightly different from the Denver stores, with larger children's, sports and religion sections, but all of the usual touches were present, including green carpet, dark brown walls, antique furnishings, coffee bar, newsstand and space for author events. The Highlands Ranch store proved popular but somewhat too large for the market. When its lease expired in April 2015, it relocated a few miles north to Aspen Grove, a popular shopping center at South Santa Fe Drive and West Mineral Avenue, anchored by Alamo Drafthouse Cinema. The mix of neighboring stores was good for

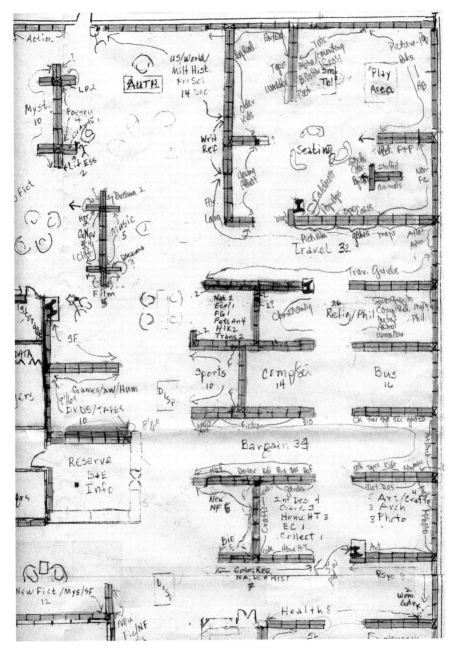

A portion of Meskis's hand-drawn Highlands Ranch floor plan, 2004. *Courtesy of Linda Millemann.*

store traffic, and the somewhat smaller space lent Tattered Cover Aspen Grove a wonderful intimacy.

In 2012, Meskis inked a deal with Hudson News, which operated several bookshops at Denver International Airport, to franchise the store's name, with one miniature Tattered Cover in the Jeppesen Terminal and in each of the airport's three passenger concourses. This was part of the airport's effort to feature more local businesses, even if operated by national companies like Hudson, to impart the flavor of Denver. These four shops put Tattered Cover's name in front of arriving passengers, who would then, it was hoped, remember to visit the larger in-town stores. The concourse locations opened in 2014 and the Jeppesen store after the terminal's remodeling.

The year 2014 also saw another new Tattered Cover in a transportation hub, this shop not franchised but owned by Meskis. In 2001, the Regional Transportation District bought Denver's Union Station, the oldest parts of which date to 1881, from its previous owners, several railroads, intending for it to eventually serve as multimodal transportation hub with rail (Amtrak and RTD's light and commuter rail lines) and regional bus service to replace Market Street Station. A consortium, Union Station Alliance, was tapped to redevelop the station's buildings and construct new ones behind and around it. The Alliance included longtime historic preservationist Dana Crawford, who had long known Meskis, to curate retail and restaurant tenants, all local names. When Union Station reopened in 2014 after a two-year renovation, there was a Tattered Cover just off the Great Hall, with its familiar green carpeting and dark brown–stained bookcases; on an exterior wall store artist Sarah Clark painted a mural of a green-carpeted room lined with books and, visible from the window, a passing train. The selection was small but highly curated to serve the travelers' needs; just outside RTD's A Line soon connected Union Station with Denver International Airport.

In June 2021, the McGregor Square Tattered Cover opened at 1991 Wazee Street, about four blocks from the LoDo store, following a symbolic transfer of books, the "Book Worm," from LoDo, beginning with Sullivan's novel. This was the first new store opened by the ownership group that took charge in December 2020, about which more follows. Triangular in plan due to the building's shape, the 6,800-square-foot store on two levels was designed by line Studio's Tim Politis. Despite its tenancy in a brand-new building instead of a century-old one, the light-filled store felt like a true Tattered Cover; incorporating areas of green carpeting, the architect also warmed the space through extensive faux wood flooring and parallel

Top: Highlands Ranch under construction, 2004.

Bottom: Joyce Meskis cuts the ribbon at Highlands Ranch, November 2004.

rows of dark-stained wooden planks hung from the ceiling, softening the raw concrete and HVAC ductwork and helping moderate the acoustics. A grand bookshelf-lined staircase with multiple landings harkened to the LoDo and Cherry Creek stairways. Wedged into the acute eastern corner, climbing these stairs felt akin to driving up Colorado's many hairpin-turning mountain highways.

Top: Highlands Ranch, looking from the front of the store looking toward the rear, 2004.

Bottom: Shelving enclosing Highlands Ranch's children's department, 2004.

In 2019, Tattered Cover announced a new suburban location in Downtown Westminster, the redevelopment of the former Westminster Mall at Sheridan Boulevard and West 88th Avenue. At this book's writing, the store, featuring Tattered Cover's first wine bar, was scheduled to open in late 2021, adjacent to the lobby of the 125-room Origin Hotel at the newly platted intersection of Westminster Boulevard and West 89th Avenue.

"Friends of Tattered Cover" shopping event at Aspen Grove, 2019.

Aspen Grove's wooden ceiling, legacy of a previous tenant, casts a warm glow, 2021.
Photograph by author.

Union Station's Tattered Cover from the train platform, 2021. *Photograph by author.*

Tattered Cover Westminster, in a corner ground-floor space (*right*) adjacent to the Origin Hotel. *Photograph by author.*

Also opened in 2021 was the first age-specific location, Tattered Cover Kids, a 1,400-square-foot mini-shop with 4,800 titles just for children. Located in Aurora at the local business–focused Stanley Marketplace, 2501 Dallas Street, it drew from the large juvenile population of Aurora and Central Park, the redevelopment of Denver's former international airport. Many of its shelves were short so small readers could reach the books, and wall murals by Patrick Maxcy "whimsically evoked the experience of getting lost in a story," per a press release. In a back corner, an abstract tree-like construction provided a space for story time. It is never too early to get the next generation of readers interested in books.

CHANGES, PLANNED AND UNPLANNED

Stanley Marketplace was the first location announced by Tattered Cover's new ownership group, but to discuss that change we must first turn the calendar back to 2015, when Meskis decided it was time to retire. Now seventy-three, she had managed the institution for more than four decades, along the way fighting for reader privacy (see sidebar), serving as president of the American Booksellers Association (ABA), directing University of Denver's Publishing Institute and winning countless awards and accolades. In March 2015, Meskis announced that Len Vlahos and his wife, Kristen Gilligan, had agreed to take over, effective July 1, 2017. A two-year transition would allow the new owners, relocating from Connecticut, ample time to learn every aspect of Tattered Cover's business. Meskis and Vlahos were not strangers; he had served twenty years at the ABA, rising to chief operating officer and leaving it in 2011 to helm the nonprofit Book Industry Study Group. Gilligan too had served in the ABA's marketing department. It had long been Vlahos's and Gilligan's dream to own a bookshop, but they never dreamed it would be Tattered Cover.

The transition began in the summer of 2014, when Vlahos and Gilligan, realizing their dissatisfaction with Connecticut's crowded roads and relative lack of outdoor recreation for their two boys, began thinking about living out west. Vlahos called Meskis to ask about Colorado opportunities, and after forty-five minutes, she asked if he would be interested in taking over Tattered Cover. After more conversations, they came to an agreement. Vlahos and Gilligan became employees until the transition, making payments over time. In July 2017, Vlahos and Gilligan assumed control after Meskis's retirement. The new team continued operating Tattered Cover

THE FIRST AMENDMENT AND TATTERED COVER

Congress shall make no law respecting an establishment of religion, or prohibiting the free exercise thereof; or abridging the freedom of speech, or of the press; or the right of the people peaceably to assemble, and to petition the Government for a redress of grievances.

It is not hyperbole to say that no one better encapsulates the connection between free speech advocacy and the operating of an indie bookstore than Joyce Meskis. No one—and I mean no one—has been a more powerful and effective advocate for free speech than Joyce, for bookstores, for the broader community here in Denver, and for the entire nation.
—*American Booksellers Association CEO Oren Teicher, 2017*

On March 17, 2000, police officers from North Metro Drug Task Force entered the LoDo Tattered Cover seeking records of a sale made to someone it was investigating. Earlier, they had raided an Adams County methamphetamine lab and found two books: *The Construction and Operation of Clandestine Drug Laboratories* by "Jack B. Nimble," and *Advanced Techniques of Clandestine Psychedelic and Amphetamine Manufacture*, by "Uncle Fester." Nearby was a Tattered Cover shipping envelope; hoping to connect these books with the suspect, the officers sought "the title and nature of any and all books" the store may have shipped in it and "any other orders placed by this customer." The officers presented these demands to Joyce Meskis, who, even though, as she later admitted, was "frightened and dumbfounded" by the situation, instinctually refused to violate the privacy of any customer, on the principle that no governmental entity has the right to know what any citizen is reading. When they persisted, she called her attorney, Dan Recht, putting him on speakerphone, and together they persuaded the officers to stand down. The task force then obtained a search warrant from Denver's District Attorney after Adams County's DA refused. Each time she was presented with a new demand or legal maneuver Meskis consistently fought to protect the right of her customers, indeed of all Americans, to read without fear of governmental oversight.

The case brought national attention, fitting a pattern: a few years earlier, independent counsel Kenneth Starr, appointed to investigate

Bill and Hillary Clinton's pre–White House dealings ("Whitewater"), had subpoenaed Washington, D.C. bookstore Kramerbooks for records related to purchases made by intern Monica Lewinsky, books given to President Clinton during the period they were conducting an affair. Several commentators compared Tattered Cover with the Kramerbooks case, but in October, Judge Stephen Phillips rejected any resemblance, ruling that "the purchase of how-to books is a highly important piece of evidence" in the prosecution of the meth lab operators and ordering Tattered Cover to turn over the records. He said Starr had been "fishing" for evidence for political reasons, while this was a case of "significant public interest" outweighing the need for privacy. The Colorado Supreme Court disagreed and in a 6–0 opinion sided with Tattered Cover on April 8, 2002, more than two years after the saga began. After the victory, Meskis declared the decision was not only a victory for Colorado book purchasers but also "an important precedent for readers, bookstores and library patrons throughout the country." This was Tattered Cover's, and Meskis's, proudest moment: the First Amendment prevailed, with national consequences. Ironically, the shipping envelope that started the inquiry had not contained the manuals at all. Instead, it had held *A Guide to Remembering Japanese Characters*, by Kenneth G. Henshall; the accused perpetrator purchased it for artwork to inspire tattoos. Recht revealed the title at a panel discussion at the Denver Press Club, a fitting venue for a coda to a consequential fight for the freedom of ideas.

along lines Meskis had established, venerating the First Amendment and maintaining it as a bastion of ideas, even if they did not personally agree with every one of them. Gilligan particularly focused on reinvigorating the store's relationship with schools, coordinating approximately one hundred in-school events to promote reading and approximately twenty to thirty in-store book fairs. All seemed well, although Vlahos and Gilligan knew the store faced challenges. Vlahos put Tattered Cover on sounder financial footing by negotiating the favorable McGregor Square and Westminster leases and mulled eventually taking on investors.

Then came Covid-19. In March 2020, the store closed to customers and furloughed many staffers—furloughing rather than laying off, so employees could keep health insurance. (Ultimately some were laid off.) Vlahos estimated that sales dropped by 80 to 90 percent in the pandemic's early

The Vlahos-Gilligan
family, with Hillary
Rodham Clinton, 2017.
Courtesy of Len Vlahos.

stages, but he regrouped, focusing on online sales for shipment or curbside pickup. Gilligan worked without pay; both toiled alongside remaining employees, often eighty to one hundred hours weekly, to get books to readers. Vlahos caught Covid and was hospitalized for five days. Colfax resembled a warehouse, with temporary pack-and-ship stations placed across the floor, employees distancing from each other. All stores reopened to in-person shopping later in the spring, keeping capacity limited and asking customers to use hand sanitizer, but without an available vaccine, many stayed home.

Then came the murder of George Floyd, a Black man a Minneapolis convenience store clerk suspected of passing counterfeit bills. The clerk called the police and set off a chain reaction that upended American race relations and politics. During past periods of political turmoil, Tattered Cover had stayed out of the fray, following the Meskis philosophy of not censoring any ideas, no matter how offensive, and conversely, not promoting ideas Meskis might have personally believed in, unless First Amendment–related.

This time was qualitatively different. To some staffers the "neutrality of ideas" was no longer the best stance to take, particularly at a time when so many community members felt pain over Floyd's death and those of other Black people. Several declared in an all-store email chain that the bookstore should respond with a definitive antiracist statement, and Vlahos agreed, composing an email to customers. "Black Lives Matter," it began, providing an antiracist reading list. Vlahos then reminded readers of the store's longtime neutrality stance, illustrating the message with examples of controversies on which it had remained neutral. Although sincere and in line with store history, it was the wrong note: there is no neutrality when it comes to racism. Several employees quit in protest, various community members and organizations commenced a boycott and more than one hundred people signed a public letter condemning the statement. Vlahos received death threats. Two days later, he sent another email, also posting it to the website, deeply and sincerely apologizing. He then expressed regret individually to staffers and hired Denver-based Prismatic Varied and Brilliant, a DEI (diversity, equity, inclusion) consultancy, to audit store practices and coach management and staff. Vlahos recognized later that he had not understood that Tattered Cover's philosophy needed to evolve to reflect its community's evolution. Vlahos and Gilligan lacked adequate funds to weather the double crisis of pandemic and boycott, even with a Paycheck Protection Program loan. Tattered Cover was clearly in danger of closing just shy of its 50th anniversary year, much as the *Rocky Mountain News* ceased publishing in 2009 just shy of its 150th. Yet the store still had fans, and they would rescue it.

Among them were David Back and Kwame Spearman. In their thirties, they had known each other since high school, sparring on their respective schools' debate teams (Back at George Washington, Spearman at East), making friends in the process. Both had embarked on ambitious business careers. After college (University of Pennsylvania and Harvard Law), Back moved to India to start that country's first large-scale, legally operating car rental company, Zoomcar. Yet he never forgot Tattered Cover, where his parents had brought him as a boy and where he landed his first job at fifteen. Spearman, growing up in east Denver, had similar experiences with his civil rights–oriented father and academically minded mother, who frequently brought him to Tattered Cover, instilling a love of reading. In high school, he enjoyed the Fourth Story whenever he could, particularly, he joked, "when someone else was paying." Spearman was president of the class of 2006 at Columbia, subsequently attending Yale Law and Harvard, where he studied and worked with Dr. Henry Louis Gates. Entering business, he began as a consultant with Bain & Company, followed by B.GOOD Restaurants and Knotel, a flexible office provider. Like Back, Spearman retained warm memories of the bookstore. It was only after he lived elsewhere that he realized not every city has a store like Tattered Cover and came to appreciate it even more when he could not just pop in.

He compared it with growing up with a view of the Rockies, something taken for granted until you live somewhere with no such vistas—not every city has a bookstore to compare with Tattered Cover.

When Covid-19 hit in early 2020, Spearman, like many New Yorkers who could afford it, left the city. Landing in serene Vermont, he reassessed and reflected. He thought about his purpose, wondering what he could say to his eventual offspring about what he had done comparable to his father's civil rights work or his mother's educational career. He and Back had long discussed how they might eventually return to Colorado, but neither perceived the state as offering the same kinds of business opportunities they were used to. In late April, Back read that Tattered Cover had furloughed part of its staff and considered talking to Vlahos about investing or even buying it outright. He wanted it to continue—it was too important to fail. He called Spearman, who initially thought him a little crazy, but as Spearman knew, "Nothing he has ever done is crazy, even if it sounds crazy." Spearman, like many, had assumed that brick-and-mortar retail was dying, but his interest was piqued and he began researching. He learned that in 2019 there were more independent bookstores than there had been in 2010, despite competition from online retailers—logically this should not be, but it was clear that brick-and-mortar bookstores still had relevance. He learned he was not alone in considering Tattered Cover an important institution, no less so than museums, libraries or performing arts organizations. He mulled over what Back proposed.

The pandemic accelerated preexisting trends, and as it became clearer that Tattered Cover was on the brink of closing if someone did not step in, Back, Spearman and Denver-based partner Alan Frosh decided to act, setting up discussions with Vlahos and Gilligan. They assembled a group composed of themselves, local investors and book industry executives, all ardently desiring to see Tattered Cover continue. They set up a cleverly named limited liability company, Bended Page LLC, to buy the store, and by December the deal was done. The new Tattered Cover organization now had a board of directors, with Back as chair. Spearman moved to Denver, bought a house in Whittier and became CEO; Frosh became chief community officer. The investors knew they were not going to become rich, but all valued the institution highly enough that they saw participating as a public service.

The reader of 2071 will know whether Tattered Cover will make it to its century mark. For the immediate future, as this is being written in the 50th anniversary year, Tattered Cover has survived the crises of 2020 and is embarking on its next stage. Shortly after taking the reins, Spearman began implementing new ideas. The first was reaching out to Clara Villarosa. In 1984, when she founded Hue-Man Bookstore, Denver's first Black-owned bookstore, she contacted Meskis, who provided advice; for the sixteen years of Hue-Man's existence, Meskis encouraged her booksellers to steer readers toward it as an important resource. She and Villarosa cohosted a conversation group called the Race Club, bridging divides between Black and white by bringing together Tattered Cover and Hue-Man customers. Villarosa, who founded the African American Booksellers Association (a division of the ABA), sold her shop in 2000, moved to New York and opened a new Hue-Man in Harlem, which lasted until 2010. Spearman recalled visiting Denver's Hue-Man; each year his family bought Black Santa Claus Christmas cards there. He arranged for the now-ninety-year-old Villarosa to curate a "Hue-Man" section at each Tattered Cover, filled with the latest and most important titles by and for Black people. Villarosa also made herself available to consult with companies and school districts seeking books on African American life and history.

Spearman recognized too that for brick-and-mortar bookstores to thrive they had to provide something special—to be "experiential," in retail jargon. While Tattered Cover has long hosted author readings and book signings, up to five hundred events per year, Spearman envisioned not only reinvigorating that program after the pandemic but also adding other events to attract community members who might not otherwise have reason to enter a bookstore: panel discussions, prominent people discussing books that had inspired them, and, recognizing that more than one-third of Denverites identify as Hispanic, Chicano or Latinx, events in Spanish. He considered opening additional Tattered Covers in underserved parts of Denver and Colorado, and to ensure that new customers could always find something affordable he increased purchases of bargain and used books. Future stores might be "segmented" toward particular markets, such as Stanley Marketplace's child focus. Spearman intends for Tattered Cover to continue as the community institution it has always been, but even more so. The idea, urge and imperative of bringing people and books together will not die.

Part Two

The Famous, the Not-So-Famous and Sometimes the Infamous

I n fifty years, Tattered Cover has hosted thousands of appearances by authors—famous authors, local authors, children's authors, writers of self-help books, writers of poetry, writers of books people remember and books they forget. People have participated in myriad other events too: Harry Potter parties; children's story time; book group seminars; June 16 Bloomsday readings of James Joyce's *Ulysses*; in-store performances by members of Opera Colorado, Colorado Symphony, and other local groups; and even sitting in the Cherry Creek store's 1st Avenue display window to read books. Kids have entered bookmark coloring and short story contests, while adults have attended series events such as Second Monday Poetry, Writers Respond to Readers, Rocky Mountain Land Series and Tattered Cover Film Series. It was not always this way in Denver: before Tattered Cover, authors might sign books occasionally in department stores or the random bookshop. Tattered Cover gave publishers a reason to send authors to Denver. Authors loved coming, knowing they would receive first-class treatment and encounter appreciative audiences. Every author was asked to sign the store's autograph books, now a collection of dozens of volumes; every author, too, was given an engraved brass bookmark as a thank-you gift. When inspirational speaker Zoe Koplowitz, famous for taking more than a day to complete the New York City Marathon but persevering despite multiple sclerosis, came to sign *The Winning Spirit: Life Lessons Learned in Last Place*, she burst into tears when presented with her bookmark, because no other store had treated her as well.

Chris and Julia (no last name given) read in Cherry Creek's 1st Avenue window, November 1992. Participants received T-shirts that read, "Reading is Alive and Well at the Tattered Cover."

Joyce Meskis looked on as former employee Linda Millemann held her gift, an engraved brass bookmark, at a signing for her poetry book, 2013.

CREATORS

Given how many immensely creative people Tattered Cover has hosted over the years, it is only fitting that its first-ever book signing occurred in late 1977 when one of the twentieth century's greatest landscape photographers, seventy-five-year-old Ansel Adams, came to sign *Natural Light Photography*. In 1982, another early guest was brilliant R. Buckminster Fuller, in his mid-eighties when he came to promote *Critical Path*. The great thinker had broken his finger, and his grandson asked for a bowl of hot water without saying why. Between signing books, Fuller soaked his hand to relieve the pain but greeted every customer and signed every book; it was only afterward that staffers learned why he wanted hot water. Another suffering author was novelist and nature writer Peter Matthiessen, who signed with a broken hand. Philosopher Mortimer J. Adler, best remembered for his "Great Books of the Western World" program, also visited Tattered Cover more than once, as did Beat poet Allen Ginsberg. Mythologist Joseph Campbell came in 1983 to sign the first volume of his *Historical Atlas of World Mythology*, five years before Bill Moyers's PBS series *The Power of Myth* made Campbell widely popular.

Dressed in his trademark white suit, Tom Wolfe visited Tattered Cover in 1979, signing *The Right Stuff*, his nonfiction account of the original seven Mercury astronauts. The store served wine, molasses cookies and naturally, Kool-Aid, recalling his earlier *The Electric Kool-Aid Acid Test*. A *Rocky Mountain News* reporter described his autograph as "almost an illustration, a bold scribble that takes off into a huge circle at the 'W' and another one at the 'f,' with the 'e' inserted as a tiny afterthought—flamboyant, but stylish, a graphoanalyst's delight." He suggested he would follow up with a novel about New York, which became his satirical *The Bonfire of the Vanities*. When Wolfe returned in 1987 to promote it, customers were told he would be signing *Bonfire* and nothing else, but when a man approached to say, "I can't afford [*Bonfire*], but I brought along the book I carried through Vietnam," *The Electric Kool-Aid Acid Test*, Wolfe broke his own protocol, signing the tattered paperback.

In 1981 Joyce Meskis hired two remarkable women on the same day, Margaret Maupin and Virginia Valentine. They had worked together at Tumbleweed Books, and both would influence Tattered Cover greatly over coming decades, growing into nationally regarded bookselling legends, with Maupin becoming frontlist buyer and Valentine fiction buyer. Maupin remembered her first day, August 1, as an exciting one, with the store hosting

Edward Abbey signed *The Fool's Progress* at Cherry Creek, 1988.

With love to all at The Tattered Cover from a tattered author.
Madeleine L'Engle.

The Tattered Cover, a warm and unexpected gem of a store.
Jonathan Dart

Tom, I mean, from a dizzy author to the mile-high bookstore, love in a cool climate,
Germaine Greer
7. V. 84.

— To my good friends at The Tattered Cover. See you again in Heaven.
Edward Abbey
May 1984

Tattered Cover has asked authors to sign its autograph books since the early 1980s; the collection now numbers dozens of volumes. Four noted authors signed this page in 1984.

John Nichols, author of *The Milagro Beanfield War*, in town to sign the third novel in his New Mexico Trilogy, *The Nirvana Blues*. The line of fans stretched from the second-floor signing desk down the stairs, out the door and around the corner; Nichols took time to chat with everyone. This would not be the last Tattered Cover signing with long lines.

When Meskis promoted Maupin to frontlist buyer, which then also meant responsibility for running author events, Maupin had reservations, worrying she was unqualified because she mostly read nonfiction. Meskis, convinced Maupin was right for the job, reassured her, and Maupin soon began devouring new novels and becoming an expert in fiction. When A.S. Byatt published her Booker Prize–winning *Possession: A Romance* in 1990 Maupin loved it and began recommending it to customers, a

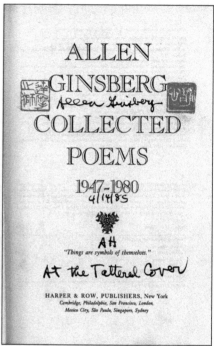

Above: Tattered Cover owned a collection of books signed by authors, usually but not always on the title page, including these by Toni Morrison and Allen Ginsberg.

Left: Maya Angelou came to the Middle Store in 1983 for *Shaker, Why Don't You Sing?*

Humorist Dave Barry, frequent Tattered Cover visitor, likely at Cherry Creek, date unknown.

Humorist Erma Bombeck at Cherry Creek in 1987 for *Family—The Ties that Bind...and Gag!*

Bloom County cartoonist Berkeley Breathed signed *Billy and the Boingers Bootleg* supervised by a stuffed "Opus" at Cherry Creek, 1987.

practice known in the bookstore trade as "hand selling." When a book is recommended enough times it can gain momentum, and Maupin's advocacy of the British Byatt's book certainly helped the author win many American readers not just in Denver but nationally, as Tattered Cover was by then influential enough that when a book became a TC bestseller other booksellers took notice. Ultimately, *Possession* sold over 100,000 hardcover copies in America, a phenomenal figure for literary fiction. (Maupin did not claim credit, telling the *Rocky Mountain News* in 2006, "I don't know if I was the push.") When Byatt toured, her publicist asked for an October 31 slot. Maupin, sure that people would not come on Halloween, resisted, but agreed due to Byatt's tight schedule. It was a cold, snowy Halloween

And what was she, the Fairy Melusine?
Men say, at night, around the castle-keep
The black air muffles 'neath the outstretched vans
Of a long flying worm, whose sinewy tail
And leather pinions beat the parted sky
Scudding with puddered clouds —d black as soot,
And ever and again a shuddering cry
Mounts on the wind, a cry of pain and loss,
And whirls in the wind's screaming and is gone.

Christabel La Motte

AS Byatt

With best wishes to the Tattered Cover,
Hallowe'en, October 31st 1991.

A.S. Byatt's entry in Tattered Cover's autograph book, 1991.

(hardly unusual in Denver), and when Byatt arrived in her limousine she came wrapped up in hat and gloves, accompanied by a suitcase full of books. She told Maupin and the good-sized audience, "I know you don't usually have signings on Halloween, so I'm going to read you a ghost story!" After the event, when she signed the autograph book, she included another wonderfully eerie verse.

When Norman Mailer came that same year to sign his 1,300-plus-page doorstop *Harlot's Ghost*, Maupin, knowing his reputation for not suffering fools, worried about conversing with him, but when he and wife Norris Church Mailer arrived the couple put her at ease; she described the occasion as "like being with an uncle, he was very gentlemanly." He

Much love to the
gang at Tattered Cover
from the gang at
28 Barbary Lane

Armistead
11 Jan 1987

Armistead Maupin, unrelated to
longtime Tattered Cover buyer
Margaret Maupin, came many
times to sign his *Tales of the City*
series and other novels.

read a passage and announced, somewhat intimidatingly, "I'll take a few questions, but I don't want any stupid ones." Few asked any. In Maupin's own copy, he wrote, "to Margaret, who has been the nicest hostess tonight, Cheers, Norman Mailer." Another towering figure that concerned Maupin before her arrival was philosopher/novelist Susan Sontag. Maupin had not found time to read *The Volcano Lover* prior to Sontag's arrival and worried that making small talk would be difficult. After the audience left, Sontag asked for wine. Maupin kept a bottle in her office for such an occasion; she brought it out, poured and Sontag kept Maupin and others entertained until one o'clock in the morning.

Kentucky writer Bobbie Ann Mason was the opposite of intimidating, her warm drawl charming audiences on regular Tattered Cover visits. Her fans turned out to hear her read from *Zigzagging Down a Wild Trail* on Monday evening, September 10, 2001. Maupin spent the following day, in the wake of what happened in New York, Washington and Pennsylvania, trying to determine the whereabouts of the author scheduled to speak that night, but on Wednesday morning she awoke and realized that Mason probably had not been able to leave town before flights were canceled. She phoned The Brown Palace, and Mason was indeed still resident, having spent Tuesday glued to the television. Maupin invited her to dine at her own home that evening with herself and husband Bruce; Mason graciously accepted and enjoyed a fine evening, telling Maupin she'd probably just buy a car, since rental agencies were cleaned out, and drive home. Longtime Tattered Cover employee Andrea Phillips remembered that week for a different reason. Working in LoDo that

The Rock Bottom Remainders, a charity rock super group composed of a varying lineup of writers and professional musicians, came in 2000 for a Denver SCORES kids' soccer fundraiser at the Gothic Theatre. After a press conference held in the Fourth Story, several signed Tattered Cover's autograph book. *Top to bottom*: Stephen King, Scott Turow, Amy Tan (and her Yorkies), founder Kathi Kamen Goldmark, Ridley Pearson and Dave Barry.

alarming Tuesday, she encountered shocked customers who said they naturally gravitated to the store; not only was it one of the few places downtown still open, but they also came because it felt like the safest place and they did not want to be alone. Tattered Cover represented normalcy in a suddenly changed world.

Dave Eggers visited Tattered Cover frequently; the store was the first in Denver to stock his literary journal, *Timothy McSweeney's Quarterly Concern*. Usually appearing at LoDo, he would visit Wynkoop Brewing Company prior to the event. After ordering a beer, he told the bartender to keep the tab open. At the book signing, he invited audience members to join him at the Wynkoop for free drinks afterward, and many did, increasing the tab to four figures. Another David, humorist David Sedaris, was similarly generous, at least to longtime events coordinator Charles Stillwagon. For years, both men smoked, often enjoying cigarettes in the alley behind

Left: Future U.S. Poet Laureate Joy Harjo signed her memoir *Crazy Brave* at Colfax in 2012.

Below: English romance novelist Jackie Collins came to Cherry Creek in 1994 for *Hollywood Kids*.

Top: Historian Doris Kearns Goodwin signed *The Bully Pulpit* at LoDo in 2013.

Bottom: Historian David McCullough signed *The Wright Brothers* at Colfax in 2015.

LoDo prior to events; during signings Sedaris told audience members they could skip to the front of the line if they gave him a cigarette. One year Sedaris quit the habit, but for Stillwagon he brought his last carton of Kool Milds, which both had favored.

In 1997, framed silkscreened pieces by writer Kurt Vonnegut adorned the LoDo Event Hall's walls. Vonnegut arrived in October to promote his final, semiautobiographical novel, *Timequake*. This was not a traditional signing—Stillwagon hauled hundreds of copies to a Brown Palace suite where Vonnegut pre-signed them—but an on-stage interview, a not uncommon

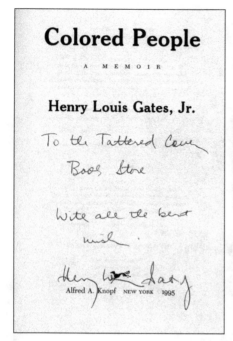

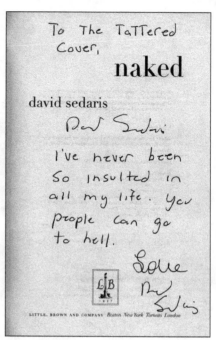

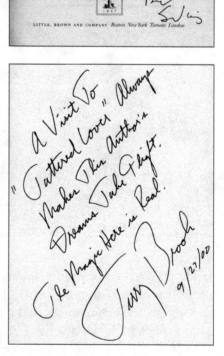

Clockwise from top, left: Historian Henry Louis "Skip" Gates Jr. signed his memoir in 1995; Humorist David Sedaris signed *Naked* in 1997; Fantasy novelist Terry Brooks visited Tattered Cover many times. He always obliged, signing anything his fans brought him, often staying well past closing time; Kurt Vonnegut came to LoDo for *Timequake* in 1997.

format for important authors' appearances. The interviewer was Wynkoop Brewing Company's John Hickenlooper. A year earlier, Vonnegut had phoned Hickenlooper, who was stunned when the caller identified himself. Vonnegut explained that he had heard of Hickenlooper through LoDo gallery owner William Havu, who was showing Vonnegut's artwork. Havu had told him of Hickenlooper's announced plans to brew "Kurt's Mile High Malt" in conjunction with the exhibition. Vonnegut asked if Hickenlooper knew whatever had happened to his Cornell University dormitory hall mate and fraternity brother in 1938, also named John Hickenlooper, and he replied, "Yeah, that was my father." Hickenlooper's parent had died when the future brewer was young, so Vonnegut filled him in on what he had been like during college. For Kurt's Mile High Malt, Vonnegut wrote a very short story, "Merlin," for the label. When *Timequake* appeared, its 44th chapter included references to Denver and Hickenlooper.

When Ayad Akhtar read former Tattered Cover employee Kalen Landow's online rave for his 2012 bildungsroman *American Dervish*, he reached out to her. He thought her review perceptive and asked if she could interview him for a Tattered Cover appearance in conjunction with the paperback release. Surprised by his reaching out, she readily agreed. He arrived during terrible winter weather, which produced a turnout of fewer than ten people. Akhtar invited the audience to form a conversation circle, a special, intimate way to discuss the book, made more so in attendees' recollections a few months later when he won the 2013 Pulitzer Prize for Drama for his play *Disgraced*. Turnout was similarly small, and for similar reasons, when first-time novelist David Guterson came in 1994 for *Snow Falling on Cedars*. Hoping to impress his Colorado-resident brother, Guterson was unhappy with the small crowd size, but could only have been pleased by Tattered Cover's selling thousands of paperback copies in subsequent years and by large turnouts for his signing of that edition and later books.

Proving that heartfelt, sometimes self-deprecating personal stories resonate with many readers, novelist/memoirist Anne Lamott attracted 1,100 to a Tattered Cover-staged event at Trinity Methodist Church in 2018 for *Almost Everything: Notes on Hope*. Typically, at Lamott's events, "fans bring her gifts, like socks printed with the face of the Virgin of Guadalupe, and M&Ms," per a *New York Times* mention of the event.

In 2020, with the Covid-19 pandemic putting an abrupt end to author tours, Tattered Cover worked hard to make up for their loss. When comic fantasist Christopher Moore's *Shakespeare for Squirrels: A Novel* came out, the

Left: Dave Eggers read from *A Heartbreaking Work of Staggering Genius* for a 2001 offsite benefit for Webb-Waring Institute, with Tattered Cover selling books.

Below: Writer George Saunders shook a fan's hand after signing *The Tenth of December* (paperback edition) at LoDo in 2014. *Photograph by Reggie Ruth Barrett.*

Gollum loves the TATTERED COVER

Thanks for a great event – I had a wonderful evening
Alan Lee 27 – 10 – 05

J.R.R. Tolkien illustrator Alan Lee visited Tattered Cover at least twice. In 2005, he drew Gollum creating tattered covers in the store's autograph book.

Top: Santa Fean George R.R. Martin travels to Denver frequently, sometimes stopping by casually to sign stock, other times at formal signing events like this one at LoDo in 2011.

Bottom: John Irving came to LoDo in 2009 for *Last Night in Twisted River*.

store created a "virtual signing line," with an online waiting room. Each person who participated got two minutes to chat with the author. After the December 2020 ownership transition, the new team worked hard to build a slate of online events; by June 2021 Tattered Cover was hosting up to thirty-five each month.

CELEBRITIES

Depending on one's definition of "famous," and probably on one's age, the most notable celebrities to appear at Tattered Cover were either Bob Hope or Arnold Schwarzenegger. Or they were Shirley Temple Black or Bruce

Springsteen. Or they were Gloria Estefan or Judy Collins or Kareem Abdul-Jabbar or Cal Ripken. Regardless of the level of fame, when big names appeared they occasioned special preparations and first-class treatment. Most stars warmly put staffers at ease, acting like normal people. When Isabella Rossellini came she introduced herself to each person working the event. Afterward she graciously thanked everyone by name, not forgetting one. Following are stories of some celebrities who have attracted large Tattered Cover crowds.

Bob Hope came twice, to the Middle Store in 1985 and Cherry Creek in 1990. On that first occasion, Hope and wife Delores signed his seventh book, *Bob Hope's Confessions of a Hooker: My Lifelong Love Affair with Golf*. At least four hundred came, one couple asking him to sign seventeen copies, which he did graciously. Many reminisced with Hope, recalling memories of his USO shows during World War II. The first Hope signing was likely the largest event to date for Tattered Cover, but more than five hundred came to his second appearance, for *Don't Shoot, It's Only Me*. People formed lines outside before 7:00 a.m. for his midday signing, bringing books and

Basketball great Kareem Abdul-Jabbar signed *Kareem* at Cherry Creek, 1990.

Baltimore Oriole Cal Ripken Jr. visited LoDo in 2004 to promote *Play Baseball the Ripken Way* to an enthusiastic audience of kids and parents. *Courtesy of Charles Stillwagon.*

memorabilia—not all celebrities will sign these items, but Hope did. When the scheduled end came at 2:00 p.m., Hope stood up, stretched and walked away, although many were still lined up; Maupin recalled that two women got into a tussle over the last signed book, which both claimed. Shirley Temple Black, by contrast, "stayed and stayed," occasionally exiting to smoke outside Cherry Creek's third-floor doors. Many fans brought granddaughters dressed as Temple had been in her 1930s films, when she was Hollywood's most popular child star.

Longtime staffers remembered the March 25, 1993 Arnold Schwarzenegger event as the most chaotic one ever. An estimated 2,500 fans came to see the Terminator, who had recently wrapped the third film in that franchise; younger fans had ditched school to spend all day waiting to hear him speak and sign *Arnold's Fitness for Kids Ages 11–14*. Staffers kept everyone waiting outside; when the doors opened, the roar of excited fans pouring in was loud enough to be audible on the third floor. Seeing him was free, but as with other large signings people needed numbers for places in line. Staff stopped handing them out after 985; ultimately 447 got their books signed.

T͟h͟e Reading Glass

Tattered Cover News & Reviews

Vol. 4 Issue 3

Bringing a World of Books Into Focus

The Tattered Cover Book Store, a Readers Haven for more than 30 years

priceless!

Prior to digital marketing, Tattered Cover published various printed newsletters, with graphic design by staff members Patty Miller and Ann Marie Martin.

Left: Joyce Meskis at 1628 Wynkoop Street, circa 1990. *Courtesy of Thomas J. Noel; photograph by Berkeley-Lainson.*

Below: Colfax Tattered Cover, 2021. *Photograph by author.*

Above: Members of Friends of Tattered Cover, the store's loyalty program, shop Colfax, 2019.

Left: Union Station's compact interior, 2021. *Photograph by author*.

Mural by staff artist Sarah Clark in the corridor leading to Tattered Cover Union Station, 2021. *Photograph by author.*

Morey Mercantile's former loading dock housed children's books, circa 2012.

LoDo's newsstand, circa 2012.

LoDo's second floor, circa 2008.

"Charlie" at LoDo, on the original Morey Mercantile staircase (closed to shoppers) between the first and second floors, circa 2008.

McGregor Square, across 20th Street from Coors Field. *Photograph by author.*

McGregor Square's children's department under the stairs, 2021. *Photograph by author.*

McGregor Square's staircase provides views of both floors, 2021. *Photograph by Lucy Beaugard.*

"Book Worm" volunteers and CEO Kwame Spearman, lower left, enjoyed McGregor Square's opening, June 26, 2021. *Photograph by author.*

Downtown's skyline can be seen from McGregor Square's second floor, 2021. *Photograph by author.*

McGregor Square's second floor, 2021. *Photograph by Lucy Beaugard.*

Aspen Grove, 2021. *Photograph by author.*

Left: Singer/poet Jewel visited Aspen Grove in 2015 for her memoir *Never Broken*.

Below: Tattered Cover Kids at Stanley Marketplace, 2021. *Photograph by author.*

Opposite, top: Stanley Marketplace's second level provides an elevated view of Tattered Cover Kids, showing Patrick Maxcy's west wall mural, 2021. *Photograph by author.*

Opposite, middle: Kids'-eye-level view of Stanley Marketplace's rear wall and "tree." *Photograph by Lucy Beaugard.*

Opposite, bottom: Stanley Marketplace's second level provides an elevated view of Tattered Cover Kids, showing Patrick Maxcy's east wall mural, 2021. *Photograph by author.*

Christopher Moore used a blue Sharpie to sign *The Serpent of Venice* at LoDo in 2014.

Tattered Cover pop-up shop for the 2021 MLB All-Star Game at Coors Field, featuring over one thousand books devoted to America's pastime. *Photograph by author.*

The alley-spanning bridge at LoDo included this piece of Morey Mercantile memorabilia, circa 2008.

Rita Skeeter (staffer Mikaley Osley), standing in front of the store-built Whomping Willow, emceed a Harry Potter trivia contest at Colfax, 2018.

President Jimmy Carter greeted people who asked him to sign *A Full Life* at Colfax in 2015; newcomer Len Vlahos (*far left*) and longtime employee Cathy Langer (*to Carter's right*) assisted.

At Colfax in 2018, former first lady Michelle Obama inspired unfettered joy.

Tattered Cover Chairman David Back, 2021.

Tattered Cover Chief Executive Officer Kwame Spearman, 2021.

Above: Tattered Cover
Chief Community Officer
Alan Frosh, 2021.

Right: Author Dave
Eggers used tempera
paints for this unique
entry in Tattered Cover's
autograph book, 2001.

Hi TATTERED
COVER.

You ARE
MY HEROES.
HERE IS
A BIRD
WITH
BAD THINGS
ON HIS
HEAD.
OR
MINE.
OOPS!

D.E.

DAVE EGGERS 3/4/01

Entertainer Bob Hope descending the Middle Store's staircase, 1985.

Astronaut John Glenn signed *John Glenn: A Memoir* at LoDo in 1999.

Chef Julia Child posed with Joyce Meskis at Cherry Creek in 1995. She signed copies of *In Julia's Kitchen with Master Chefs* along with her classic two-volume *Mastering the Art of French Cooking*.

Those hoping for a glimpse stood on desks and tables and even climbed bookshelves. Longtime general manager Matt Miller, possibly the calmest, most unflappable person ever born, lost his temper and yelled at people to stop climbing bookcases, which would not support them, and in fact, one, the peace and non-violence section, collapsed. When Schwarzenegger left, store manager Neil Strandberg, tasked with getting him to the elevator, turned his arms into a "cow-catcher" to plow through. Looking over his shoulder, Strandberg saw people reaching to touch the star and heard him greeting delirious fans. The day proved a valuable learning experience.

When *Breaking Bad* star Bryan Cranston came to Aspen Grove in 2016 to sign *A Life in Parts*, the atmosphere was far calmer, even though, with nine hundred, it was still a large event. It took place at nearby Alamo Drafthouse Cinema, with Cranston interviewed in one auditorium and a video feed to the others. Two years later, Sally Field came to promote her memoir *In Pieces*, attracting a similar number. An "amazingly sweet lady" per the event's coordinator, everyone who came met and greeted her, posing for photos with

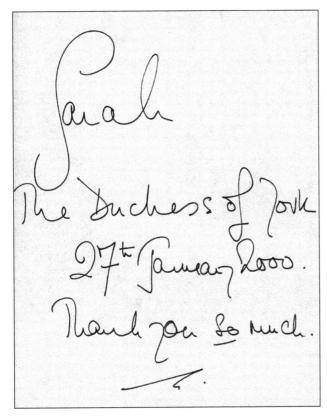

Left: Sarah, Duchess of York, was "perfectly lovely" to Tattered Cover staff, per event coordinator Charles Stillwagon, when she visited LoDo in 2000 to promote *Win the Weight Game*.

Below: Actor and East High School graduate Pam Grier came to LoDo in 2010 to sign her memoir *Foxy*. *Courtesy of Charles Stillwagon*.

Actor Val Kilmer appeared at Cherry Creek in 1987 to sign his limited-edition poetry collection *My Edens After Burns*.

the woman who portrayed such diverse roles as Sister Bertrille in *The Flying Nun* and Gidget to Norma Rae and Mary Todd Lincoln.

Born to Run was the natural title for Bruce Springsteen's 2016 autobiography. One of rock's biggest stars, his book became a massive bestseller, and every bookstore coveted a spot on his extremely limited tour, initially just nine stops. This would not do for Len Vlahos. In what he later described as a "wonderful bonding experience" with staff, he created a direct video pitch to Springsteen called "Come to the Tattered Cover, Bruce!" Sitting in his basement office at Colfax, he began by recounting how he got his first guitar in 1978 and learned to play songs by his favorite acts, including Springsteen. He described once playing in a Jersey Shore bar band as he left his office, accompanied by his wife and their two children, picked up a guitar and began strumming and singing the lyrically dense "Growin' Up," from 1973's *Greetings from Asbury Park, N.J.*, which he obviously knew well. As Vlahos walked through receiving and offices, employees joined him, carrying homemade signs. The parade emerged into the children's book section, climbed the stairs and wended through the main floor, ending at the "stage" just as Vlahos finished singing. In

Actor Valerie Harper was all smiles at LoDo in 2001 when she signed *Today I Am a Ma'am.*

British professor and singer Will Kaufman brought his "live documentary" format to Colfax in 2011 when he came to sign *Woody Guthrie: American Radical. Photograph by Reggie Ruth Barrett.*

Canadian singer-songwriter Bruce Cockburn posed with a fan when he came to Highlands Ranch in 2014 for his memoir *Rumours of Glory. Photograph by Reggie Ruth Barrett.*

unison, between thirty and forty employees implored Springsteen to come, and it worked. The event felt like a party, with five hundred ecstatic fans who had pre-purchased his book meeting their idol and posing for pictures with him.

THE BEST LAID PLANS

Planning for author appearances usually began months in advance with staff collaborating with publishers and publicists to ensure the signing went smoothly. Sometimes, however, events intervened out of everyone's control. For instance, when Gene Hackman, who came to LoDo in 2004 to sign *Justice for None*, the National Weather Service issued a tornado warning for Denver. The crowd disappeared, leaving Hackman to chat amicably with employees sheltering in the basement. Then there was actor Joan Collins, scheduled for a lunchtime signing, also at LoDo. Her plane was two hours late, and by midafternoon the audience had evaporated to just one very dedicated person; Collins remained cheerful about it. Mystery writer Mary Higgins Clark was booked to appear jointly with daughter Carol Higgins Clark but slipped on a banana peel (truly) the day before. Forbidden by her doctor to fly, she appeared via speakerphone. *CBS Evening News* anchor Dan Rather canceled his appearance for his memoir *I Remember* in early 1991 when a United States–led coalition invaded Kuwait—he had to cover the start of the Persian Gulf War. He came back for a later book, however.

It worked the other way too, with writers endeavoring to honor their commitment even when their schedule-following publicists wanted them to get to the airport. Besieged by more fans than she anticipated, photographer Annie Liebowitz, slated to depart in the afternoon, remained signing books for several hours. "There are people here to see me and I'm not leaving until we're done," she insisted. For an evening event, Caroline Kennedy's flight was delayed by weather. She attracted hundreds, who waited patiently until after the store closed. Kennedy finally arrived and signed books into the wee hours. As the daughter of a book editor, she was an avid reader who always looked forward to discussing books and spent a lot on tomes to take home.

Behind the scenes at LoDo, actor Gene Hackman posed for a photograph by a member of the store's cleaning crew, June 9, 2004. *Courtesy of Charles Stillwagon.*

Left: Rosanne Cash read and signed *Composed: A Memoir* at LoDo in 2011. *Photograph by Reggie Ruth Barrett.*

Right: Filmmaker/activist Michael Moore asked Tattered Cover for a Flint, Michigan branch when he signed the autograph book.

Comedian Chelsea Handler was booked into LoDo for a daytime signing on the Saturday of Denver's massively attended St. Patrick's Day parade. That event and associated traffic kept her from reaching the store on time, spending hours in a limousine. The audience, meanwhile, had already been celebrating the traditional way, imbibing Guinness and other adult beverages at local watering holes. When she finally arrived, she immediately realized the effect. "You're drunk!" she announced. "I'm the only one here who's sober!" Because it was St. Patrick's Day weekend, the event got even more interesting. Handler counted among her fans many little people due to her *Chelsea Lately* television show sidekick Chuy Bravo, who had dwarfism. An adult entertainment venue near the convention center traditionally booked little people as "stripper-leprechauns" that weekend, and an enthusiastic contingent came to see Chuy's friend Chelsea.

Country singer Rosanne Cash came in summer 2000 to sign her children's book *Penelope Jane: A Fairy's Tale*—it was not a formal book tour, but since she was to perform an evening concert at Fiddler's Green, her publicist arranged for an early afternoon appearance. It was a weekday, not ideal for a daytime event; employees put out fifty chairs anticipating a good-sized crowd, but when it was clear that fewer than ten people had come, the staff began quickly putting chairs away so Cash would not encounter an embarrassing sea of empty seats. She arrived while they were doing this, but instead of complaining about the crowd's size she pitched in to help, and instead of standing at the podium she told audience members to put their chairs in a circle and spent an hour informally chatting with them about *their* lives and interests. Cash returned a different year for a different book, also coinciding with a concert, this time at Denver Botanic Gardens. Prior to the Tattered Cover event, she asked for a quiet room where she could phone into NPR's *Wait Wait...Don't Tell Me!*, the weekly news quiz show, as she had been booked as a guest.

Another author booked for an event with a national media tie-in was Michael Moore. He was just signing books, not speaking, so instead of Colfax's downstairs event space the staff put his table upstairs on the "stage," near the reserve desk, so camera operators could use the store's cavernous, book-filled interior as backdrop for his appearance, halfway through the event, on MSNBC's *The Rachel Maddow Show*. Event planners informed thrilled customers they might be seen on national television. Besides selling Moore's books, the store got free advertising, which never hurts.

ODDITIES AND ANECDOTES

Writers bring their eccentricities with them on book tours. Denver's Hotel Monaco advertises itself as pet-friendly, offering guests a goldfish to take up to their room. This captivated novelist T.C. Boyle, who gladly accepted the offer when he checked in. He then disappeared for several hours, and the event staff began to wonder if he was coming, but he finally arrived. He had spent his day combing downtown, looking for a pet store so he could buy an identical goldfish to put into the bowl, hoping to convince hotel staff that spontaneous parthenogenesis had resulted in their goldfish asexually reproducing. Had the big downtown Woolworth still existed, he might have succeeded in his quest.

Tom Robbins, best known for novels aimed at adults, came to Tattered Cover in 2009 to sign what was ostensibly a children's book, *B is for Beer*. He brought along a bag of Mary Jane candies, an old-fashioned peanut butter and molasses confection. As each person reached the desk he unwrapped

One of Chuck Palahniuk's props. *Photograph by author.*

a piece, half-chewing it while signing. Then he took the candy out of his mouth, placed it in the book, and slammed it shut. No one ever knew why, and he would not say, but it made for interesting, if sticky, memories.

"Transgressional fiction" writer Chuck Palahniuk liked to send, in advance, props for audience members to interact with. Once he sent a crate of blow-up dolls and asked fans to compete to inflate them the fastest. For another event, the store received a box of rubber dog toys in the shape of severed bloody limbs. Sometimes no props were needed to make things exciting: he had a short story, "Guts," he said was short enough that it would last only as long as audience members could hold their breath. As he toured the country, reports emerged of dozens of people fainting after taking the challenge. Forewarned, the store took action, lowering the thermostat and bringing in giant fans to keep air circulating—and nobody at the Tattered Cover event fainted.

Other authors did not bring blow-up dolls or severed arms, but nicer things. Singer Naomi Judd came with guardian angel nightlights, handing one to each child who came for *Naomi Judd's Guardian Angels*, a picture book. Local mystery writer Diane Mott Davidson (who had featured Cherry Creek's business section's "hidden room" in one novel) brought cookies she had baked; her books typically incorporated food-related themes. Canadian cookbook writer and television host Bob Blumer (*The Surreal Gourmet*) arrived at LoDo in 2000 driving an Airstream camper resembling a giant toaster with two large slices of "toast" on the roof. Coming to sign *Off the Eaten Path: Inspired Recipes for Adventurous Cooks*, he fired up the Airstream's grill and began cooking crustaceans, serving them to random passersby. Plated with them were dolls: he called it "shrimp on the Barbie."

Sometimes food was served *to* authors, such as when Colorado-based thriller writer Stephen White's first book, *Privileged Information*, appeared in

Laurie "Arrgh" King's pirate-themed birthday cake at Colfax, 2011. *Courtesy of Charles Stillwagon.*

1991 and his family ordered a sheet cake decorated with its cover. When mystery writer Laurie R. King was booked at Colfax for a September 19, 2011 signing for *Pirate King*, staff learned it would be her fifty-ninth birthday and asked if she wanted to celebrate. She loved the idea, asking, since the plot involved Gilbert and Sullivan's operetta *The Pirates of Penzance*, for a themed party, so the store ordered a pirate-themed cake, eye patches, black tricorne hats and even a stuffed parrot that hung near the podium. The author had hoped for a sing-along ("Hurrah for our Pirate King! / And it is, it is a glorious thing / To be a Pirate King."), but that did not happen.

Writers sometimes brought canine friends with them on tour. Local author Pam Houston used to arrive with her very large wolfhound. Novelist and children's author Amy Tan came on several visits with Yorkshire terriers, which surprised the audience by popping out of her handbag; other times they would lie quietly at her feet. Jane Fonda brought a young puppy, instructing event staff to give it just enough water to keep it hydrated but not enough to fill its bladder because she did not want it piddling on the carpet. Novelist James Salter arrived with a Welsh corgi as old in dog years as he was in human years. Marcia Clark, lead prosecutor in the O.J. Simpson murder case and author of several mysteries along with her account of the Simpson

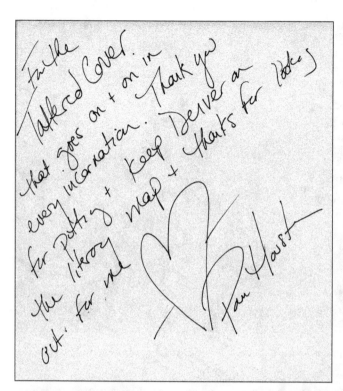

For the Tattered Cover. that goes on + on in every incarnation. Thank you for putting + keep Denver an the library map + thanks for Books out for me ♥ Pam Houston

Left: Colorado author Pam Houston has loved Tattered Cover for years, buying others' books and signing her own.

Below: Writer Amy Tan (*right*) and illustrator Gretchen Schields (*left*) sign copies of *The Moon Lady* at Cherry Creek in 1992.

trial, was startled when a tiny dog jumped out of an audience member's purse and ran across the signing table.

Unseen by customers, Cherry Creek had two stairways for emergency egress and fire department access. In 1995, on tour for *My Life in High Heels*, *WKRP in Cincinnati* star Loni Anderson was interacting with fans on the third floor when suddenly Denver firemen poured out of the hidden stairs. No, there was no fire or fire alarm—they just wanted to meet her, but in the middle of their shift they could only make an "official" visit—the public stairs would not do. Years later, British explorer and storyteller Redmond O'Hanlon was visiting LoDo to sign *No Mercy: A Journey into the Heart of the Congo*. The lights were lowered, and he regaled the audience with slides of indigenous people he had met and creatures he had encountered. He spoke of the importance of healers, pulling out a talisman, a small wooden doll he had been given, used in healing. Just at that moment, as he described the doll's latent power, the fire alarm went off—no fire, but uncanny timing on the doll's part. When firemen found no fire, he posed for pictures with them and the doll, standing in front of their truck.

Whitley Strieber came to Tattered Cover with an air of otherworldliness, thanks to decades of writings about interactions with "the visitors." He maintained these episodes had left him "altered" and predicted to event staff that the sound system would fail. It did. It had performed properly during the previous event, and it worked fine for the subsequent one, but when Strieber began speaking the speakers erupted in howling feedback, then cut out entirely. This happened twice, once in Cherry Creek and again in LoDo. Coincidence?

POLITICOS

Inviting politicians to sign books can risk alienating some subset of customers, depending on whether authors have a D or an R after their names. Protesters can show up. Security measures can be strict. For much of its history, Tattered Cover has gladly welcomed the extra work presented by these kinds of events, because it is important for democracy that people be allowed to meet their political heroes—or in the case of one quiet older liberal, to politely tell conservatives she came to see that she disagreed with them, sometimes handing them a written statement explaining why.

This page: President Jimmy Carter signed *An Outdoor Journal* at Cherry Creek in 1994 (*top*) and posed with staff at another Cherry Creek event for *Talking Peace* in 1993 (*bottom*).

Jimmy Carter was easily the most prolific ex-president, authoring or coauthoring over thirty books since leaving the White House, and he visited Tattered Cover more than any politician who was not from Colorado, signing books and greeting well wishers in the 1980s, 1990s, 2000s and 2010s. Gracious to staffers and the public alike, the president known for his warm smile was also a master at signing books, approximately ten per minute, but always making eye contact and acknowledging each person; in 1995 he signed 1,055 copies of his poetry collection, *Always a Reckoning*. As with many famous signers, his publicists set rules forbidding memorabilia, but at one event he was presented with a photograph showing the American Embassy staff in Tehran before the Iranian Revolution—the man had been a hostage during Carter's presidency. Carter looked up, recognized him, quietly uttered "oh!" and signed it.

Hillary and Bill Clinton have appeared at Tattered Cover several times. In 1996, when Hillary Clinton published *It Takes a Village: And Other Lessons Children Teach Us*, two thousand people who had pre-purchased the book were given numbers for places in line to meet her. The Secret Service prescreened select staffers; non-screened employees were forbidden from accessing Cherry Creek's third floor on the day. The first and second floors densely filled with people prior to her arrival; one brought a Labrador retriever, in training as a service dog, which heeded the call of nature amid the crowd (staffers, including the author, formed a barricade until it was cleaned up). Antiabortion advocates staged pickets on the 1st and Milwaukee corner, met by counter-protesters, including "Bitches for Hillary." The event ran smoothly. The first lady arrived on time, waving to supporters as her limousine came around the corner from 1st Avenue, then entered the garage and ascended the elevator (the left-hand one opened on two sides, allowing VIPs to arrive unseen).

Senator Clinton returned in 2003 for her memoir *Living History*, this time signing about 1,500 books by hand instead of the autopen used for *Village*. In 2014, anticipating a presidential run, she came for *Hard Choices*, her memoir of her secretary of state years, and returned in 2017 after winning the 2016 popular vote but not the Electoral College for *What Happened*, her account of that election. For her supporters, feelings remained as raw as they had been on November 8, 2016, including those too young to vote. When introduced to Clinton, Len Vlahos and Kristen Gilligan's son Luke, then seven years old, looked up at her and said, "I wish you were president." She dropped to her knees so she could look him in the eye and replied, "I do too." She accompanied daughter Chelsea Clinton to Denver for a Tattered Cover–staged talk and signing in 2019 at the Paramount Theater, attended by

This page: Hillary Rodham Clinton appeared at Cherry Creek's lower level event space in 2003 (*top*), and at Colfax in 2017 (*bottom*).

1,800, for *The Book of Gutsy Women,* in which both were interviewed by local author Helen Thorpe.

When Bill Clinton came in 2004 to sign *My Life,* two thousand people showed up at LoDo to greet him—a number then-marketing director Heather Duncan said was a predetermined upper limit to prevent chaos. The event could have been much larger, probably the largest in Tattered Cover's history, so great was demand. His people had provided a list of personal guests expected, including his spiritual advisor and Denver-area resident Carlotta Walls LaNier, one of the "Little Rock Nine," the first Black students to enroll at Little Rock Central High School in 1957. Clinton was standing near the bridge to the Event Hall when the elevator door opened and LaNier emerged. The two fell into each other's arms; manager Derek Holland whispered to events coordinator Charles Stillwagon, "We're witnessing history." To force him to sign books quickly Clinton requested that jazz play in the background, but he still chitchatted with everyone who came; one woman said he made her "feel like I was the only person in the world." Clinton ignored protesters outside.

Two years later, junior senator from Illinois Barack Obama came to LoDo to sign *The Audacity of Hope* and paperback copies of *Dreams from My Father,* attracting a diverse crowd of over eight hundred. Employees watched from the alley loading dock as a convoy of black limousines pulled up. Obama emerged, waved at everyone and asked for a trash can for his chewing gum

President Bill Clinton posed with staff in LoDo's Event Hall in 2004.

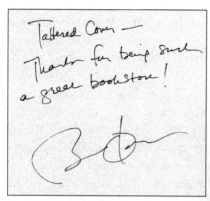

Future president Barack Obama spoke in
LoDo's Event hall in 2006.

as he entered; more than one staffer considered whether it would one day
have monetary value if they were to save it. Upon entering the Event Hall,
the future president immediately noticed a group in wheelchairs clustered
near the dais; it was the store's practice at large events to reserve a spot in
front for people in wheelchairs. Obama greeted them, knelt down to sign
books and listened to their stories. The event consisted of an interview by
then-mayor John Hickenlooper, followed by a signing line. Many walked
away after meeting him hoping he would become America's first Black
president, and two years later their wishes came true.

A decade later it was time for the Obamas to write their post-presidential
memoirs. Michelle Obama, famously, completed and published hers,
Becoming, first, in late 2018 ahead of her procrastinating (and wordier)
husband. Given her status and popularity, the tour was booked into sports
arenas, including Denver's Pepsi Center, where she had spoken during the
2008 Democratic National Convention. Local stores bid for the right to
sell books at that event, and Boulder Bookstore won. Yet Tattered Cover's
consolation prize was arguably better than winning would have been: a
personal appearance at the Colfax store, where five hundred tickets (which
sold out in seven seconds) allowed fans to meet and greet the inspirational
former first lady, a thrill beyond measure to many.

Tattered Cover has hosted former cabinet members, including Secretaries
of State Madeleine Albright, John Kerry and Condoleezza Rice. Albright

At Colfax in 2018, former first lady Michelle Obama posed with staff.

had close associations with Denver, where she attended Kent School, where her sister still lived and where her father, Josef Korbel, had founded University of Denver's Graduate School of International Studies, later renamed for him. It was there that Rice obtained her doctorate in 1981. Albright gave extemporaneous talks at her Tattered Cover appearances, some held in store and others at Trinity Methodist Church. KMGH-TV anchor Bertha Lynn interviewed Rice on stage at LoDo. Before he was secretary of state, and just after serving as chairman of the Joint Chiefs of Staff during the Persian Gulf War, General Colin Powell came to Cherry Creek in 1995 to sign his memoir, *My American Journey*. Would he or wouldn't he, American journalists wondered, run for president against Bill Clinton in 1996? Given his stature and popularity, the publisher staged a press conference in the Fourth Story, at which Powell did *not* answer that question. Anticipation of just such a historic announcement brought about four thousand people to the store, however, generating massive sales. Powell managed to sign several hundred books, but schedule commitments forced him to leave before hundreds more people got theirs signed; event staff learned much from that event.

A few years earlier, the other major figure to emerge from the Persian Gulf War, General Norman Schwarzkopf, set a Tattered Cover record

Secretary of State Madeleine Albright in LoDo's Event Hall on two different occasions in the early 2000s.

Vice President Dan Quayle's signing line for *Standing Firm* spiraled down Cherry Creek's stairs in 1994.

when he signed 1,375 books in three hours and three minutes. People began lining up at 3:10 a.m., beginning with a Marine lieutenant colonel who had fought in Operation Desert Storm; people drove hours to meet Stormin' Norman. Former vice presidents have attracted large Tattered Cover crowds too, including Dan Quayle and Al Gore, who came more than once. Former first lady Barbara Bush came to Cherry Creek in 1994 to promote *Barbara Bush: A Memoir*. The store was filled with her fans, and when a page came over the PA system requesting, "Barb Bush, please come to the first-floor counter," it startled many—why would someone page a first lady? Staffers assured everyone that Barbara Bush was also the name of a Tattered Cover general manager.

Anyone who lived in Denver during August 2008 has memories of the city's brief transformation into the epicenter of American politics when it hosted the Democratic National Convention. The LoDo Tattered Cover, thanks to its location near Pepsi Center, large downtown hotels and MSNBC's temporary broadcast stage at 16th and Wewatta Streets, was in the thick of it. The parking lot abutting the Otero Building sprouted "The Big Tent," sponsored by DailyKos and other progressive entities to house political bloggers. The store rented the Event Hall to *National Journal*, the Washington, D.C.–based weekly political news magazine. It used the hall as hub for its journalists and presented political panel discussions each morning. Writer Michael Chabon, covering the convention for *New York Review of Books*, also popped in that week.

During that month, Tattered Cover also hosted the Speaker of the U.S. House of Representatives, Nancy Pelosi, who signed *Know Your Power: A Message to America's Daughters*. Because she was third in the line of presidential succession, security had to be especially tight, nearly equal to a presidential visit. The Speaker, however, does not get Secret Service protection, so Pelosi traveled with members of the Capitol Police, which serves the legislative branch. Denver Police closed the alley below the Event Hall, blocking it with multiple vehicles, and the store hired local security expert Marcus Fountain to assist. Attendees were required to buy the book. This included people who detested Pelosi, hoping to confront her. Anticipating potential disruption, the staff used zip ties to connect folding chairs together in rows so they could not be thrown. As she spoke, multiple people made attempts to rush the stage, but they were rapidly nabbed and taken away. Pelosi, used to this sort of thing, shrugged it off; that evening she attended a Rockies game with her daughter Alexandra.

Left: Michael Chabon returned to LoDo in 2012 for *Telegraph Avenue*.

Right: Onetime presidential candidate Reverend Jesse Jackson signed *Legal Lynching* in 1996 after delivering remarks in LoDo's Event Hall.

Speaker Nancy Pelosi posed with staff at LoDo in 2008.

COLORADO AUTHORS

Despite what coastal literati might have thought when the city was younger, Denver has long been home to nationally prominent men and women of letters, including Eugene Field, Damon Runyon, William MacLeod Raine, Mary Coyle Chase, William Barrett and others; had Tattered Cover been around then it surely would have hosted them. Here are a few of the many Colorado authors who have appeared at the store.

Novelist and historian Sandra Dallas has shopped at Tattered Cover for its entire existence and has signed "at least a dozen" of her books there. She recalled, "Whenever Margaret Maupin or Lisa Casper introduced me, they made me feel like I was the greatest author to ever enter the store. It seemed the Tattered Cover had signings every day, but the two always knew details about the author and the author's personal life. Tattered Cover employees genuinely care about books and authors." Shopping, she remembered a bookseller instantly knowing she was looking for Caleb Carr's *The Alienist* when she asked for "a murder mystery about a doctor"; at a chain bookstore she had previously visited the clerk just shrugged, knowing nothing of the bestseller. Another time, she sought travel guidebooks on Greece. The bookseller handed her several, gave recommendations and told her to sit at a desk and take notes if she liked.

Local historian Thomas J. "Dr. Colorado" Noel treasures memories of dozens of Tattered Cover book signings, beginning in 1978 with *Richthofen's Montclair*. "Here I was, an obscure author with a book on an obscure topic who would sell only a few books, hosted by one of the country's... most famous book stores! I remember Joyce's soft, warm sweet voice[,] like talking to your grandmother." His friend Dennis Gallagher came to many of his signings, to "do a blessing—in Latin—on book buyers, on Joyce Meskis, and on the TC." For Noel's official history of the Denver Archdiocese, "Dennis blessed the book with an impressive sounding *Nihil Obstat* and *Imprimatur* that...the Church used to put on books to which it had no objection." Phil Goodstein, Denver's own Howard Zinn, also premiered many of his copiously researched history tomes at Tattered Cover, to audiences of appreciative local history fans.

Newspaper columnist Woody Paige was interviewing novelist Clive Cussler on the radio when Margaret Maupin heard him complain that Tattered Cover had never invited him to sign books. She immediately contacted his publisher, obtained his phone number and asked him to come, the first of many times. The *Raise the Titanic!* author lived in the

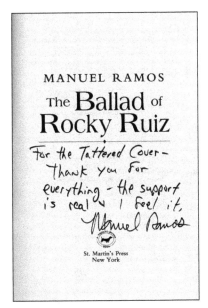

MANUEL RAMOS

The **Ballad** of

Rocky Ruiz

For the Tattered Cover -
Thank you for
everything - the support
is real & I feel it,
Manuel Ramos

St. Martin's Press
New York

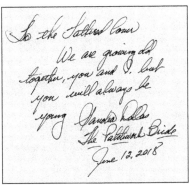

To the Tattered Cover
We are growing old
together, you and I. but
you will always be
young *Sandra Dallas*
The Patchwork Bride
June 12, 2018

Top: Local "Chicano Noir" novelist Manuel Ramos signed his first novel, *The Ballad of Rocky Ruiz*, at Cherry Creek in 1993.

Bottom: Denver author Sandra Dallas signed books at Colfax in 2018 and many times before, there and at earlier Tattered Cover locations.

Denver area and preferred to sign books on Saturday afternoons, when the store was at its busiest. He would arrive at Cherry Creek and without ceremony sit down at the third-floor signing desk, and start—no reading or talk beforehand. Lines snaked downstairs and around the first floor.

Woody Creek–based Hunter S. Thompson proved a problematic Tattered Cover guest on just one occasion. Booked to sign at LoDo, the notorious gonzo journalist had to be pulled unwillingly from Oxford Hotel's Cruise Room to appear on schedule. He arrived inebriated and became more so as the evening wore on, having procured a bottle of whiskey from the bar. The store knew he would smoke and provided an ashtray. Meeting fans, he offered swigs of booze if he liked them; if he did not he pretended to burn them with his cigarette. Two brothers came, and he accidentally (?) burned one. They left but returned, asking Thompson to re-create the burning for a photograph. At that point, the sober event staff stepped in and reminded everyone that Thompson was subject to a court-ordered curfew and had to return home. Those who worked with Thompson never forgot that night.

Kent Haruf was a Colorado author beloved by store staff, and he felt the same way about Tattered Cover. Former frontlist buyer Cathy Langer remembers him as "humble and kind," that "it was a gift to know him." The store's championing of his spare, affecting novels about the fictional town of Holt, Colorado (based on Yuma), such as *Plainsong*, led to strong sales locally, which translated

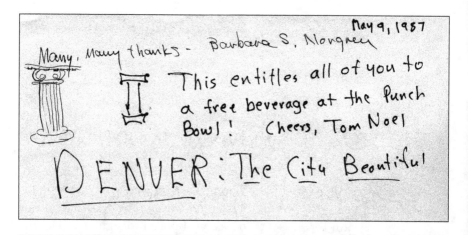

Top: Colorado historian Thomas J. Noel coauthored 1987's *Denver: The City Beautiful* with Barbara S. Norgren, signing at Cherry Creek.

Bottom, left: Denver historian Phil Goodstein's 1999 autograph after a LoDo event praised Tattered Cover as an oasis of culture.

Bottom, right: Denver writer Helen Thorpe's autograph, like those of many local authors, heaped praise on Tattered Cover.

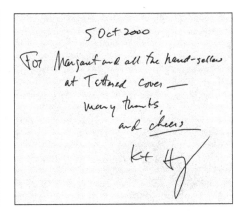

To the Tattered Cover,
I'm so sorry I stole
from you ONCE.
I owe you money.
Love,
Adam Cayton-Holland

5 Oct 2000
For Margaret and all the hand-sellers
at Tattered Cover —
many thanks,
and cheers
Kt Hf

Left: In 2018, Denver comedian Adam Cayton-Holland signed *Tragedy Plus Time*, admitting a youthful indiscretion in the TC autograph book.

Right: Colorado writer Kent Haruf acknowledged Tattered Cover's championing of his books when he signed the paperback of *Plainsong* in 2000.

Longtime Denver concert promoter Barry Fey signed his memoir *Backstage Past*, along with concert memorabilia, at LoDo in 2011. *Photograph by Reggie Ruth Barrett.*

Singer and East High School graduate Judy Collins signed *Sweet Judy Blue Eyes: My Life in Music* as well as memorabilia at LoDo in 2011. *Photograph by Reggie Ruth Barrett.*

into national momentum. He signed books at Tattered Cover on several occasions, and the Salida resident always made a point to stop by, say hello and sign stock when visiting Denver.

CHILDREN'S AND YOUNG ADULT AUTHORS

Dear Tattered Cover,

I took my 9-year-old son and two of his friends to your book signing and lecture by Brian Jacques last week. What a blast! Jacques was boisterous, irreverent, and hilarious, much like his Redwall characters, who my son adores. My son even left the lecture saying that he would now consider becoming a writer when he grows up (so he could, as Jacques put it, scribble in other people's brand new books and not get in trouble). Thank you for arranging and hosting this event. It offered us a chance to meet a real hero (Jacques is our family's version of a rock star) and laugh continuously for a solid hour. You provide a great community service through all your events, and our city benefits from your presence.

Thanks again,

Anne Button, Denver

Children's books are possibly the most important any bookstore sells; instilling a love of reading among the young is crucial to child development and societal health. Tattered Cover has always provided a large selection for young readers (with Stanley, an entire store!) and generated excitement around reading in other ways, sponsoring story and bookmark-coloring contests and hosting book fairs in-store and in schools. Every Tattered Cover except Union Station has included a space for story time, with books read either by staff or visiting authors. One employee relished warm memories of seeing Tomie dePaola at Cherry Creek when she was seven. Illustrator Michael Hague came to Tattered Cover many times too, always creating a whimsical drawing for each person—the line moved slowly, but art takes time. When Allen Say came to sign the Caldecott Medal–winning *Grandfather's Journey*, about his ancestor's immigration from and return to Japan, he drew his grandfather in each book he signed. Tattered Cover also once hosted illustrator Jon J Muth, who brought supplies to demonstrate his artistic method to young readers.

No children's author has proven more popular in recent decades than J.K. Rowling. She arrived in Cherry Creek's lower level on Saturday, October 24, 1998, for a 10:30 a.m. reading and signing of *Harry Potter and the Sorcerer's Stone*. Just fifteen people came—the last time she would have drawn a crowd that small. By the second and third Harry Potter books, she was too busy writing to tour, and the reserve desk overflowed with preordered books when official publication dates arrived. Publishers establish publication (lay-down) dates for every book, but for particularly big titles they are especially strict about not allowing sales beforehand; a store could lose first-day rights for subsequent books, potentially a huge penalty. Thus were born the Harry Potter midnight parties. For book four, *Harry Potter and the Goblet of Fire*, the lay-down date was Saturday, July 8, 2000. On Friday evening, Cherry Creek began filling with families, many children wearing Harry's round glasses or scarlet and gold Gryffindor robes, along with adult Harry Potter fans. All cast hungry eyes at dozens of cartons of books stacked high behind the counter. The atmosphere was festive, with face painters applying lightning bolts to foreheads and other entertainments. At precisely midnight, a manager cut open the first carton and began selling; the last sales did not occur until after 1:00 a.m. The store sold 1,500 copies in the book's first eighteen hours.

At future Harry Potter lay-down parties, Tattered Cover developed a faster system, customers pre-purchasing the book and receiving a "Flourish and Blotts Prepaid Muggle Book Voucher" to be exchanged at midnight. By

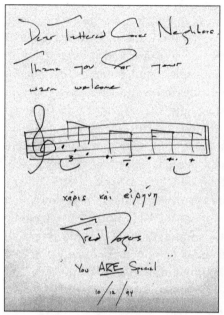

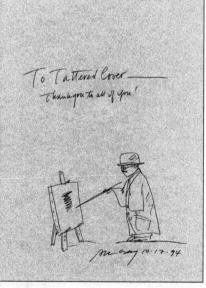

Clockwise from top, left: Children's television star Fred Rogers signed *You Are Special*, aimed at adults, at Cherry Creek in 1994; In 1995, Michael Hague returned to Cherry Creek to sign *The Book of Dragons*, illustrating the store's own copy as carefully as he did for his fans; Allen Say drew his grandfather in the store's copy of *Grandfather's Journey* in 1994; The store's newsletter announced a 1981 Maurice Sendak appearance.

Tomie dePaola entertained children on Cherry Creek's third floor in the early 1990s.

the time the final volume, *Harry Potter and the Deathly Hallows*, arrived on July 21, 2007, the stores had the process fine-tuned. At Colfax, which attracted nearly 3,000, the garage filled by 9:00 p.m. and staffers directed traffic to East High School's lot. Attendees who had been eleven when Harry was eleven in *Sorcerer's Stone* were now in college but came anyway, eager to read the story's end. Youngsters filled the time until midnight engaging in myriad planned activities, mostly staged in the "Junior Esplanade" between the store and garage. There was a Sorting Hat; "Ogg's Owlery" (an origami station); Quidditch tryouts for the "TC Tornadoes," a hoop tossing game; photo opportunities to pose for "Wizard" and "Quidditch" trading cards; a potion-making station called "Slug Club Potions Lab," where kids assembled messy concoctions of baking soda, vinegar and various natural ingredients; and "Transfiguration" (face painting). "Trivia Wizards" roamed the crowd, and the coffee shop became "The Three Broomsticks," where young or old wizards could partake of "Polyjuice Potion" and "Butterbeer." Coffee bar manager Jackie Blem concocted

In 1983, illustrator Michael Hague sat at children's book buyer Matt Miller's desk in the Middle Store to sign and draw in copies of several of his titles.

these liquid treats. Simultaneously, another 2,500 crowded into Highlands Ranch, with similar festivities. At a 2005 LoDo lay-down party for *Harry Potter and the Half-Blood Prince*, kids entered the Event Hall through a "Fat Lady" painting; once inside they could play with a giant chess set or pose for pictures on a broomstick set against a blue sky background. Tattered Cover's resident artists, Sarah Clark and Bret Bertholf, crafted these pieces. In 2018, Colfax and Aspen Grove hosted well-attended twentieth-anniversary parties with trivia contests and live owls.

Jeff Kinney, author of the *Diary of a Wimpy Kid* series, always attracted large crowds when he came to Tattered Cover. At one event, with over three hundred attendees, he arrived with his brothers, who all signed books with him, even though they were not the authors—a close-knit family in action. In March 2021, Kinney reinaugurated Tattered Cover's in-person events after a year with none by appearing at Aspen Grove for *Rowley Jefferson's Awesome Friendly Spooky Stories*. The store set up a drive-through "graveyard" in the parking lot, complete with blacklights, strobes and smoke. Attendees were encouraged to dress up cars with *Wimpy-* or *Spooky-*themed signs and decorations, with a boxed set of *Awesome Friendly* books awarded to the best one. Kinney dressed as an undertaker, and as each vehicle came by he used

Children's Events

Date **Sat. Oct. 24**   Time **10:30**   Location **CC LL**

Type Of Event **Speaking + signing**

Guest **J.K. Rowling**

Publisher **Scholastic**   Rep **Roz Hilden**

Contact **Kris Moran 212-343-7710**

Book Featured **HARRY POTTER AND THE SORCERER'S STONE** **# Ord.**

Price $ **16.95**   ☐ Hbk   ☐ Pap

Other Titles _____

Date Order Placed _____

Treats _____ Server _____

Promotion/Advertising

☐ In Store Flyer (Quantity____)   ☐ Display   ☐ Entry Easel

☐ Press Release   ☐ Newsletter   ☐ Rumpus Review   ☐ Co-Op

☐ Ad   Publication _____ Date _____

Comments **She is a tremendously popular author in Britain making her US debut**

Left: Event planners used these forms to communicate details of every signing to other staffers. On this one for J.K. Rowling in 1998, note the Comments section at the bottom, explaining who she is. On the reverse someone wrote, "We sold 9."

Below: *Harry Potter and the Deathly Hallows* lay-down party and costumed partygoers at Colfax, 2007.

Above and opposite: The "Fat Lady" painting by staff artist Sarah Clark guarded the entrance to the ~~Gryffindor Common Room~~ LoDo Event Hall (*above*); inside, staffer Bret Bertholf entertained the junior set in front of the "broomstick photo op" he and Clark built for the *Harry Potter and the Order of the Phoenix* lay-down party (*opposite*), 2005.

a gravedigger's shovel to hand signed books to excited readers, maintaining social distance during the Covid-19 pandemic.

Another crowd pleaser was Christopher Paolini. The then-teenaged wunderkind author toured the country in 2002 promoting his self-published fantasy Eragon. He dropped into Tattered Cover wearing "an elf suit," composed of "red shirt, billowy black pants, lace-up boots, and a jaunty black cap." Following store policy of not hosting self-published authors, the event coordinator said no when he asked for a signing slot. Eventually, Knopf noticed Eragon after author Carl Hiaasen's stepson raved about it, republished it under that imprint, and launched a bestseller. Cherry Creek then hosted Paolini when he toured, attracting five hundred fans. For his next book, two thousand came; he patiently signed every copy until the last reader left.

Attracting young adults to events was not always easy, so event planners had to get as creative as they did for children's authors. Beth Wood developed a game show format, "Booked," for authors to engage with teens. The rules were simple: an audience volunteer rolled a pair of dice, and depending on the outcome either the volunteer or author got to ask

questions based on Die No. 1. Die No. 2 made things silly: it forced an author to wear a beard or a blindfold while answering the posed question, flap their arms like a chicken or read their book in Pig Latin. It worked for local YA author Denise Vega, and word got around—other authors began asking for "Booked" events. Vega is one example of a local writer Tattered Cover helped promote early in her career, but there were others, including Julie Anne Peters, whose 2004 *Luna* was the first YA novel from a major publisher to feature a transgender protagonist, and picture book author Caroline Stutson. Authors, both Colorado-based and from elsewhere, knew Tattered Cover's buying and events staffs were reading their books for juveniles, hand-selling them as the store had always done for adult authors, and appreciated it.

When Stephanie Meyer's *Breaking Dawn* premiered on August 2, 2008, the store held a midnight release party similar to the Potter events. Meyer had twice previously appeared at Tattered Cover to sign earlier volumes, attracting 750 the first time and 850 the second; at the latter, Wood recalled talking to two high school girls from Greeley who told her they felt like misfits. Wood told them to look at the crowd: "Here's a whole room full of people who like the things that you like. You're not alone." When Meyer came to sign *Breaking Dawn*, the store rented East High School's capacious auditorium to handle the crowd. For the party, Wood collaborated with

Left: Author/illustrator James Gurney wrote his own Tattered Cover origin story when he came to sign *Dinotopia: The World Beneath* in 1995.

Right: Young adult writer Gary Paulsen signed for a young reader at Highlands Ranch, circa 2010.

Young adult novelist Judy Blume signed *Here's to You, Rachel Robinson* at Cherry Creek in 1993.

Neil Patrick Harris signed the second volume of his *Magic Misfits* series at a Tattered Cover event at Alamo Drafthouse Cinema Sloan's Lake, 2019.

the coffee bar's Jackie Blem on vampire-themed edibles like "bleeding cupcakes" and dreamed up questions for a trivia contest.

In 2018, Tattered Cover hosted Australian author Markus Zusak, whose 2005 *The Book Thief* generated endless arguments: was it for adults or young adults? His new work, *Bridge of Clay*, about five boys dealing with their father's disappearance, similarly appealed to both groups. The venue was Cherry Creek High School, where he would speak in an auditorium. He arrived thirty minutes early and talked one-on-one with students, curious about their lives and interests. That same year, Littleton High was the venue for a Tattered Cover–sponsored appearance by Hank Green for his debut novel, *An Absolutely Remarkable Thing*. The brother of John Green (*The Fault in Our Stars*) spoke to 550 students about his humorous speculative novel concerning robots, mysterious clues and viral celebrity.

As Tattered Cover did to attract Bruce Springsteen, employees also made a video in 2019 to invite actor Neil Patrick Harris to sign *The Magic Misfits: The Second Story*, part of a four-volume series that combines his love of magic with kids who are different, and he came. Response was huge, so the store booked all eight auditoriums at Alamo Drafthouse Cinema Sloan's Lake. Len Vlahos interviewed Harris in the largest, with a video feed into the others. Harris performed magic tricks, and the store conducted a raffle. The affable Harris signed books, and everyone who came left happy.

EVENT SERIES

In addition to individual author events, Tattered Cover sponsored event series, often with multiple authors appearing, creating a dialogue between writers, thinkers and Coloradans. These went deeper than half-hour talks at book signings, inspiring participants to think more critically about literature and many other topics.

Fiction buyer Virginia Valentine came home from Paris with an idea. At the Sorbonne, she had taken classes where writers appeared in daylong seminars and thought the idea would work in Denver. She proposed it to Joyce Meskis, who agreed. In the beginning, these January events were in-store (LoDo's Event Hall), but as they grew they moved to the Oxford Hotel. They were not free, costing $50–$65, reservations required due to limited space. The 2005 schedule was typical. Registration began at 8:45 a.m., with participants served breakfast. Valentine welcomed writers and readers at 9:15, followed immediately by author Jennifer Haigh. After a break Edward Jones spoke, followed at noon by Kent Haruf. After lunch, Vyvyane Loh spoke, followed by Peter Carey. The store served wine and cheese to send everyone home. Another, more elaborate version was a three-day affair, beginning with a cocktail reception Friday evening, followed by Saturday author appearances including Amy Bloom, Pam Houston, Jo-Ann Mapson, Jo Ann Beard and David Foster Wallace ("like dropping a James Joyce–like person into a garden party," Valentine quipped). On Sunday, it wrapped up with a book club discussion with store buyers and publisher representatives. (Valentine was also responsible for the store's book club program). The event gave Tattered Cover even more prestige among authors and publishers.

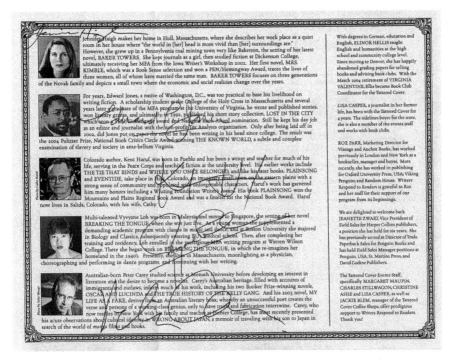

All five authors signed this Writers Respond to Readers flyer, 2005.

The Rocky Mountain Land Series was the brainchild of former longtime bargain book buyer Jeff Lee and his wife (and fellow TC employee), Ann Marie Martin. On a United Kingdom vacation in the 1990s, they encountered Gladstone's Library at St. Deiniol's, in Hawarden, Flintshire, Wales. This temple of books, established by William Gladstone and comprising the National Memorial to W.E. Gladstone, is a "residential library," a large house filled with books where scholars reside while conducting research. Returning home, they founded Rocky Mountain Land Library with a large collection (between forty and fifty thousand volumes) they had amassed, "global in scope and [crossing] all genres and subjects that explore the relationship between humans and nature." Establishing a 501c3 nonprofit, they acquired South Park's Buffalo Peaks Ranch and rented space for an urban outpost in Globeville. When Cherry Creek relocated to Colfax, Meskis donated shelving, making the library feel very much like Tattered Cover. In 2001, with the institution established, Lee inaugurated the Rocky Mountain Land Series, which

—THE ROCKY MOUNTAIN LAND SERIES—

The Rocky Mountain region has experienced unprecedented growth in recent years. As our population grows, and the demands on the environment increase, there has never been a greater need for us to know the land at our feet. The Tattered Cover Book Store, in partnership with the Rocky Mountain Land Library, has established a series dedicated to the study of the Western landscape. The Rocky Mountain Land Series, spanning the disciplines of Western History and the Natural Sciences, has been designed to promote a greater awareness of our home region.

Lyle Estill
Biodiesel Power
Saturday, April 29, 3:00 pm, LoDo

Lyle Estill will join us to discuss his new book **Biodiesel Power: The Passion, the People, and the Politics of the Next Renewable Fuel**, a chronicle of an emerging green industry. Whether we are nearing the end of oil, or the end of inexpensive oil, this renewable vegetable-based fuel will be a much needed energy choice in the years ahead. This special Land Series program is co-sponsored by CU Biodiesel (www.cubiodiesel.org), a nonprofit organization dedicated to advancing the use and knowledge of biodiesel.

Michael Pollan
The Omnivore's Dilemma
Tuesday, May 23, 7:30 pm, Cherry Creek

Please join us as Michael Pollan, author of the bestselling **The Botany of Desire**, discusses his latest book **The Omnivore's Dilemma: A Natural History of Four Meals** (Penguin Press, $26.95), an extremely thoughtful look at the food choices each and every one of us make, and the effect they have on our health, and the heath of our environment.

David Muench & Ruth Rudner
Our National Parks
Thursday, June 1, 7:30 pm, LoDo

Award-winning photographer David Muench and author Ruth Rudner will present a slide talk based on their latest book **Our National Parks**, a spectacularly beautiful look at seashore, glacier, mountain, desert, forest, and prairie — all protected within our National Parks.

Please note the location of each event.
All events are subject to changes beyond our control.
For up-to-date information call our Event Line at
303-322-1965 ext.7446.

Anthony Flint
This Land
The Battle Over Sprawl
& the Future of America
Saturday, June 10, 2:00 pm, LoDo

Veteran journalist Anthony Flint will discuss his new book **This Land: The Battle for Sprawl and the Future of America** ($24.95, Johns Hopkins University Press), a revealing portrait of our sometimes conflicted relationship to land and community. **This Land** tells the untold story of development in America, and shows ways to more vibrant and livable communities. This special Land Series event is co-sponsored by the Trust for Public Land. "This important book is spot-on in its analysis of America's deepening land use problems and refreshingly upbeat in its account of win-win solutions arising around the country. Flint's fingertip knowledge of detail is especially to be admired." —E.O. Wilson

Doug & Andrea Peacock
The Essential Grizzly
Saturday, June 17, 2:00 pm, LoDo

Doug and Andrea Peacock will present a slide talk based on their new book **The Essential Grizzly**, the most comprehensive chronicle of human-grizzly interaction ever written. Doug Peacock is a renowned grizzly bear expert, and the author of **The Grizzly Years**. Andrea Peacock is one of the new rising author/journalists of the American West, having written **Libby, Montana: Asbestos & the Deadly Silence of an American Corporation**.

Tattered Cover Book Store
Historic LoDo 16th & Wynkoop 303-436-1070
Cherry Creek 303-322-7727
Highlands Ranch 303-470-4050
Event Line 303-322-1965 ext.7446 1-800833-9327
www.tatteredcover.com

A 2006 flyer for the Rocky Mountain Land Series, showing the diversity of its topics.

brought hundreds of authors to Tattered Cover over several years, reading from books and conducting workshops, covering "topics as spirited as water in the West, wolf reintroduction, mining history, green architecture, and the power and persistence of Native American sacred sites." Per Lee, the series was meant "to keep the conversation on the land alive, creating a welcoming forum for both readers and writers to come together in a spirit of honest exploration."

Tattered Cover Film Series was another long-running event beginning in 1998. Howie Movshovitz, director of Film Education at University of Colorado–Denver, had previously established free community film series for Silverton and Gunnison and thought Denver should have one too. He approached Meskis with his idea, and she agreed to host it in LoDo's Event Hall. With his encyclopedic film knowledge and lively speaking style, Movshovitz provided brief talks to educate filmgoers prior to the monthly screenings, which encompassed the entire history of cinema. Selections were eclectic—he brought films from UCD's film library along with others from the Criterion Collection. A typical crowd of about one hundred included enthusiasts of all ages and backgrounds who appreciated the opportunity of seeing something significant and discussing it thoughtfully. Sometimes the program would be composed of short films such as *Regen* (*Rain*), a 1929 Dutch documentary by Joris Ivens and Mannus Franken consisting of shots of Amsterdam in rain. Movshovitz screened full-length films too, including *The Browning Version* (1951), one of Michael Redgrave's finest performances; Jean-Luc Godard's French New Wave *Breathless* (1960); the 16mm 1940 Technicolor version of *The Thief of Baghdad*; and the 1965 Jason Robards–Martin Balsam comedy *A Thousand Clowns*. Eventually, the series moved offsite to the Tivoli on Auraria Campus and later to Sie Film Center, adjacent to the Colfax store, with a small entry fee charged. *Westword* called the series "another one of those modest but vital events, steady as a heartbeat, that keeps the classics alive."

Evil Companions was the curious name for an annual literary event. The tradition began even before Tattered Cover existed, stemming from a group that met daily at the (now demolished) Auditorium Hotel bar. They adopted the name "Evil Companions," discussed literature and likely everything else over lunch and drinks and grew into a large assemblage. In the 1970s it faded away, but Dana Crawford remembered it. She approached Meskis with the idea to revive the name and emphasis on convivial literary discussion, and the two established the annual Evil Companions Literary Award beginning in 1993. Crawford co-owned the

Jacqueline Marie White
2006 Winner
18th Annual Bookmark Contest
5th & 6th Grades
Vail Mountain School

Tattered Cover
Book Store
Colorado
Colfax Avenue 303-322-7727
Historic LoDo 303-436-1070
Highlands Ranch 303-470-7050
www.tatteredcover.com

Winners of Tattered Cover's annual bookmark coloring contest got to see their work printed in color.

Oxford Hotel, the natural venue, and over the years the event, with what Meskis described a "lavish spread of food and drink," grew as it honored with cash awards the likes of Jim Harrison, Dorothy Allison, Annie Proulx, Kent Haruf, Richard Ford, Sandra Cisneros and others; entry ($50 per person) proceeds went to deserving organizations such as Denver Public Library.

Tattered Cover has also hosted many series for children and young adults. One of the longest running was the Children's Festival, begun in 1983, an all-day affair with authors, costumed characters, storytellers, music and dance and refreshments. This series eventually ended, but when Len Vlahos (a young adult author himself) and Kristen Gilligan took over operations, they revived it in 2018 with the Colorado Children's Book Festival. Partnering with OMG BookFest, a "circus-themed interactive experience of games, activities, and reading created by four middle-grade authors that visits underserved communities," per Bookweb.org, the two-hour event featured nineteen authors stationed at tables throughout the Colfax store, upstairs and down. Four, Avi (Edward Irving Wortis), Lauren Myracle, Kim Tomsic and Todd Fahnestock, were Coloradans. Gilligan told *Bookselling This Week*, "The attendees were blown away....the authors couldn't have been more gracious with everyone. It was easy to see they were enjoying being silly and interacting with the kids."

CLOSE ENCOUNTERS

LoDo's longtime western clothing purveyor Rockmount Ranch Wear takes pride in the many celebrities who have worn its stylish snap-button western shirts, its walls lined with photos of customers Bob Dylan, Paul McCartney,

Jack White and others. Tattered Cover has long attracted famous visitors too, but other than a few famous incidents, its celebrity stop-ins have not been widely publicized.

In 1988 Jimmy Carter came to sign books. Promoting a Denver gallery show of her late husband John Lennon's artwork, Yoko Ono wanted to meet Carter. Arriving at the store, she and her bodyguards ascended the stairs, passing people who held numbers for places in line. She approached Carter and was nearly stopped and chastised by an employee who did not recognize her. Carter knew exactly who she was, though, and warmly greeted her; their meeting made *The Denver Post*'s front page. A year later, Michael Jackson was in town. Hearing of Tattered Cover's vast children's selection, he decided to visit, arriving during regular hours. Everyone instantly recognized him, so he left. His people called the store: could he shop after hours? There was a debate—the store had never done this for anyone—and the consensus was that he could come. Arriving at 9:00 p.m., Jackson was given a personal tour by general manager Matt Miller, an expert in children's literature; Jackson spent several hundred dollars, and the story made the papers.

Another highly covered visit occurred in 1995, when President Clinton dropped into LoDo to shop while visiting Denver for other reasons. He already knew Tattered Cover, having shopped Cherry Creek in 1992 during his first presidential campaign, when his crew "couldn't get him out of it." Midmorning on September 20, the store received a phone call from the Secret Service: the president, accompanied by Governor Roy Romer, would arrive within thirty minutes. No one could be told. When Clinton arrived, customers would be allowed to leave, but nobody was to be admitted. A twenty-five-car motorcade stopped traffic, and although it was raining, passersby could not help but stop and gape as Clinton entered. Bookseller Joan Walker, a fellow southerner with a warm drawl and deep book knowledge, escorted him as he selected four titles: Clive Cussler's *Inca Gold*, Andrew Kimbrell's *The Masculine Mystique*, Robert Wright's *The Moral Animal* and Ivan Doig's *Dancing at the Rascal Fair*, the latter two recommended by Romer.

LoDo, being downtown, attracted famous people in Denver for various reasons. In the spring of 1997, those working evening shifts knew not to bother a certain attorney when he haunted the history section; he came frequently, seeking refuge from media attention, since he spent his days defending domestic terrorist Timothy McVeigh in a federal courtroom. With Pepsi Center nearby, musicians shopped between afternoon sound checks and evening concerts; one staffer who considered himself the world's biggest

This page: President Clinton shopped at LoDo in 1995 (*top, photograph by Official White House Photographer Robert McNeely, courtesy TC Archives*) and again in the early 2010s (*bottom*).

Tom Waits fan was speechless when Waits popped in. Bruce Springsteen and wife Patti Scialfa waved to appreciative fans when they came by sometime in the late 1990s or early 2000s. One employee recalled working at the second-floor information desk when she looked up to see John Cleese standing there. The British funnyman had a long list of books, and she spent a half hour checking inventory at other Tattered Cover stores, searching Google and ordering out-of-stock titles for someone she described as "so approachable and kind." Tall, blue-eyed Peter O'Toole attracted customer stares one December Saturday afternoon when, sitting near the coffee bar, he stood up, strode to the counter and asked for Cormac McCarthy's *All the Pretty Horses*, which was fortunately in stock in hardcover, his preferred format, even though it was already out in paper.

In the late 1990s, Cherry Creek employees, particularly sci-fi fans, realized that yes that really was *Fahrenheit 451* author Ray Bradbury sitting in the coffee shop. After a whispered discussion—dare we approach him?—one brave person asked if he would sign his books. Bradbury, in Denver for a gallery event for a science fiction illustrator, happily complied, chatting amiably with his TC fans.

During that period, with the Fourth Story attracting all sorts, one evening the store's manager on duty, Tom Rowan, received a call. Joyce Meskis was upstairs, and she asked Rowan to please take care of Edward Albee, who was finishing dinner and wanted to find a book. Rowan, with a lifelong passion for theater, a master of arts in theatrical directing and budding playwright, was floored: of course he was happy to take care of the author of *Who's Afraid of Virginia Woolf?*, but he was wearing a potentially embarrassing garment: a souvenir sweatshirt adorned with the logo of the schmaltzy Andrew Lloyd Webber musical *Sunset Boulevard*. Bravely, Rowan greeted Albee at the third-floor elevator door, hoping he would not notice his attire. Albee sought an edition of T.S. Eliot's *The Waste Land* with annotations by Ezra Pound, and Rowan, after not finding it on the shelf, searched *Books in Print*, the multivolume reference utilized prior to widespread Internet searchability. Unable to find references to Pound, Rowan remembered that, "Albee was very gracious and I could tell he was starting to feel guilty about how much time I was spending on the search," but he "probably didn't realize that TC-style customer service came with the expectation of…thoroughness even if the customer wasn't a world-famous playwright!"

Colorado politicos made frequent Tattered Cover shopping trips. In the 1990s, Governor Roy Romer sought bookseller Dottie Ambler's recommendations whenever he came for casual shopping. For Christmas

Before widespread Internet use, Tattered Cover booksellers relied on the multivolume *Books in Print*, published annually, with supplements, and kept sets scattered throughout the store. Fiction buyer Virginia Valentine stands behind an unnamed bookseller, early 1990s.

presents, he contacted buyer Cathy Langer, setting an appointment when he could shop with her for his large extended family. He would arrive with a long list, about thirty, to buy for, and Langer helped him select a book for each. Former senator and presidential candidate Gary Hart was often found shopping; staffers knew not to make a big deal of his presence. In 1980, on the morning after he won a particularly tight reelection bid, he showed up at the Old Store, casually browsing history books. In the 1990s, a frequent Cherry Creek presence was avuncular, white-haired former Denver mayor James Quigg Newton (served 1947–55), who came for a near-daily *New York Times* fix. He would pick up the paper and hand a dollar to whoever was present at the newsstand that day.

Coda

Festivities

No account of Tattered Cover's history would be complete without mentioning the many times its stores were settings for purely fun events. The holidays were always festive, the stores packed with shoppers. For several years, Denver Center Theatre Company's Jamie Horton appeared each December for a dramatic holiday reading at LoDo. Every Christmas Eve during the flush years, employees found custom Tattered Cover gifts in their staff mailboxes—a watch one year, a hoodie another, once even a wool blanket embroidered with "TC." In return, staffers celebrated the holiday by planning a gift for Joyce, the most memorable being a quilt, each square crafted by a different employee. At the close of business on December 24, Meskis presided over a gathering of staff and customers, serving hot cider. Employees celebrated at other times too, particularly Halloween.

You Are Cordially Invited
to attend the Sixth Annual
Jamie Horton Holiday Reading
for revelers of all ages
Tuesday, December 21, 7:00 pm
at the Tattered Cover LoDo store
Come and Enjoy a cup
of Hot Chocolate or Cider, some Cookies,
and a good story in the spirit of the season

Advertisement for Jamie Horton's annual holiday event, 2000.

For years, the store hosted a party, usually with live entertainment by bands Mahatma Bambi or Monkey Siren (featuring the store's own Bret Bertholf). Revelers wore costumes based on books—general manager Matt Miller once came adorned with a turned wooden stick and cut-out pictures of bodybuilders, calling himself "the Dowel of Physiques," a play on Fritjof Capra's *The Tao*

Above: The 1995 holiday gift to Joyce Meskis, each square designed by staffers. *Courtesy of Margie Keenan.*

Opposite: Colfax's entry dressed for the holidays, date unknown.

of Physics. Sometimes things got out of hand; Cherry Creek manager Neil Strandberg once mounted a table to dance, causing it to collapse. The next morning, he sheepishly encountered Joyce Meskis, his boss. "Do we need to have this conversation?" she asked. "No, I don't think so," he replied, and went back to selling books.

Bibliography

Books

Barnhouse, Mark A. *Lost Department Stores of Denver*. Charleston, SC: The History Press, 2018.

Lee, Jeff, ed. *The Landscape of Home: A Rocky Mountain Land Series Reader*. Denver, CO: Bower House, 2018.

Noel, Thomas J., and Amy B. Zimmer. *Showtime: Denver's Performing Arts, Convention Centers and Theatre District*. Denver, CO: City and County of Denver Division of Theatres and Arenas, 2008.

Smiley, Jerome C. *History of Denver*. Denver, CO: Sun-Times Publishing Company, 1901.

Author Interviews and Emails

Ashe, Christine, Facebook Messenger communication, July 18, 2021

Bertholf, Bret, email July 21, 2021

Clark, Sarah Wroe, emails July 18 and July 19, 2021

Dallas, Sandra, email July 11, 2021

Duncan, Heather, interview June 2, 2021, and subsequent emails

Laird, Roy, interview June 10, 2021

Landow, Kalen, interview June 22, 2021, and subsequent email

Langer, Cathy, interview June 9, 2021

Lee, Jeff, interview June 4, 2021, and subsequent email

Martin, Ann Marie, interview June 4, 2021
Maupin, Margaret, interview June 16, 2021, and subsequent email
Meskis, Joyce, interview June 24, 2009
Millemann, Linda, interview June 8, 2021, and subsequent email
Miller, Matt, interview June 4, 2021, and subsequent emails
Miller, Patricia, interview June 4, 2021, and subsequent emails
Movshovitz, Howie, interview July 19, 2021
Noel, Thomas J., email June 8, 2021
Osley, Mikaley, interview July 1, 2021
Phillips, Andrea, interview June 24, 2021
Rainbolt, Katherine Rose, email, July 30, 2021
Rowan, Tom, emails May 30, 2021, June 17, 2021, and July 25, 2021
Spearman, Kwame, interview June 11, 2021
Stillwagon, Charles, interview June 27, 2021, and many subsequent emails
Strandberg, Neil, interview June 19, 2021
Vlahos, Len, interview June 3, 2021
Wood, Beth, interview July 14, 2021, and subsequent emails

Newspapers and Magazines

Bookselling This Week. "Fear Visits the Tattered Cover." April 17, 2000.
Denver Post. February 26, 1984 (*Contemporary* magazine); March 16, 1990; August 28, 1990; October 8, 1994; September 21, 1995; December 24, 1995; February 8, 1996; October 9, 1996; January 25, 1998; October 21, 2000; April 9, 2002; April 16, 2003; July 27, 2003; November 14, 2004; February 7, 2007; April 13, 2007; May 27, 2012; September 23, 2014; March 6, 2015; August 23, 2015; July 1, 2017; August 22, 2019.
New York Times. July 17, 1987; October 27, 2018.
Rocky Mountain News. October 25, 1979; February 4, 1990; August 1, 1990; August 28, 1990; September 22, 1990; October 7, 1992; October 21, 1992; January 23, 1993; March 26, 1993; June 12, 1993; May 14, 1994; February 7, 1995; September 21, 1995; May 4, 1996; September 4, 1996; October 7, 1997; October 9, 1997; April 13, 2000; April 15, 2000; August 27, 2000; August 9, 2002; June 21, 2003; October 24, 2003; July 21, 2004; January 27, 2006; June 17, 2006; December 30, 2006; July 25, 2008.
Westword. May 10, 2012; March 13, 2014; July 29, 2015; January 13, 2017; June 16, 2017; December 28, 2018; March 19, 2020; February 11, 2021; March 15, 2021.

Online Media

Aldridge, Christen. "The Hue-Man Experience Returns to Denver through Tattered Cover Partnership." Five Points Atlas. https://www.fivepointsatlas.com/stories/the-hue-man-experience-returns-to-denver-through-a-tattered-cover-partnership.

American Booksellers Association. "Joyce Meskis and the First for First Amendment Rights: A Look Back." July 7, 2017. bookweb.org/news/joyce-meskis-and-fight-first-amendment-rights-look-back-36380.

Button, Liz. "Three Literary Festivals Premiere Over Single May Weekend." American Booksellers Assocation. May 23, 2018. bookweb.org/news/three-literary-festivals-premiere-over-single-may-weekend-104556

Facebook. "Come to the Tattered Cover Bruce!" https://www.facebook.com/tattered.cover/videos/10153719192830064/.

Rocky Mountain Land Library. landlibrary.wordpress.com/about/.

Shelf Awareness. "Denver's Tattered Cover Sold to Investor Group, Becomes Largest Black-Owned U.S. Bookstore." December 10, 2020. shelf-awareness.com/issue.html?issue=3885#m50830.

Simpson, Kevin. "The SunLit Interview: Clara Villarosa's Hue-Man Experience Finds Unexpected New Life." *Colorado Sun*, March 13, 2021. coloradosun.com/2021/03/13/the-sunlit-interview-clara-villarosa-hue-man-experience/.

Wikipedia. "Christopher Paolini." en.wikipedia.org/wiki/Christopher_Paolini.

Author Index

About the Author

Denver native Mark A. Barnhouse worked at Tattered Cover from September 1994 through March 2000, in Cherry Creek and LoDo. A graduate of the University of Colorado–Denver, double majoring in history and English, he has researched and written about Denver's history for twenty-five years. His most recent books include *Vanished Denver Landmarks, A History Lover's Guide to Denver* and *Lost Department Stores of Denver*; see ArcadiaPublishing.com for a full listing. He is available for talks and is a member of one of Denver's oldest history groups, the Denver Posse of Westerners. Find him on Facebook: "Denver History Books by Mark A. Barnhouse."

When the author joined Tattered Cover in September 1994, a member of the personnel team took this photograph.

Tattered Cover
Book Store
Denver, Colorado

*"The love of learning,
the sequestered nook
and all the sweet
serenity of books"*
—Longfellow

Cherry Creek 1st & Milwaukee (303) 322-7727
Historic LoDo 16th & Wynkoop (303) 436-1070
(800) 833-9327 TDD/V (303) 320-0536
www.tatteredcover.com
Convenient shopping hours seven days a week.

Tattered Cover

est. 1971   Denver, CO

*Books are
humanity
in print.*
-Barbara Tuchman

Colfax Ave. 303-322-7727
Aspen Grove 303-470-7050
McGregor Square 303-436-1070
Stanley Marketplace 720-420-5437

tatteredcover.com

Left, a bookmark from circa 2000 incorporated the Book Sense logo, a program to help independent bookstores sell books and distinguish them from chain and online competitors. Right, Tattered Cover's bookmark in 2021.

Visit us at
www.historypress.com